THE LURKING KEATS

Geraldine Pederson-Krag

UNIVERSITY
PRESS OF
AMERICA

LANHAM • NEW YORK • LONDON

Copyright © 1984 by Geraldine Pederson-Krag and Julie Castle

University Press of America,™ Inc.

4720 Boston Way
Lanham, MD 20706

3 Henrietta Street
London WC2E 8LU England

Printed in the United States of America

Library of Congress Cataloging in Publication Data

Pederson-Krag, Geraldine.
   The lurking Keats.

   1. Keats, John, 1795–1821–Criticism and
interpretation. I. Title.
PR4837.P33   1984   821'.7   83–25923
ISBN 0–8191–3788–X (alk. paper)
ISBN 0–8191–3789–8 (pbk. : alk. paper)

All University Press of America books are produced on acid-free
paper which exceeds the minimum standards set by the National
Historical Publications and Records Commission.

Introduction

A poem can be regarded in so many ways. We can react to the melody of its sounds as if we were humming a tune. We can delight in what it makes us see, as though we were strolling through a picture gallery. We can even meditate upon why the particular situation or feeling it presents seems so cogent, even though ostensibly it has not been our own experience.

As Freud said, "We laymen have always wondered greatly...how that strange being the poet comes by his material." The wish to identify with an admired writer by echoing or rephrasing his works is often taken as an incentive for writing poetry, but this is insufficient to provide the motivation for such arduous labor and dedication. What is needed is an urge which drives the poet beyond the demands of daily life. This urge is likely to have originated in a bygone time, when the poet's personality had not yet matured. Additionally, the impetus may stem from new developments otherwise too painful to face.

Although I have greatly admired and unsparingly used the research and scholarship of commentators on the life and works of John Keats, I have ventured to differ with them on the origins of his poetic inspiration. To find the "source, bright, pure and undefil'd/whence gush the streams of song" has led many critics to examine the accessible aspects of Keats' life—the location of his dwellings, the influence of his friends, the career of his uncle, the books he read. Yet emotions and memories, often unrecognized by the poet himself, were vital to Keats' creativity. By correlating his verses with his emotional development, I hope to demonstrate that Keats brought into being a secondary identity, antithetical to his ostensible personality and often asynchronous with his age, in which his genius took form and flowered.

Table of Contents

Chapter I

In 1818 a young Londoner, John Keats, and his friend Charles Brown made a pilgrimage to the birthplace and tomb of the Scottish poet Robert Burns. Keats commented, "We can see horribly clear in the works of such a man his whole life as if we were God's spies."[1] In the years since, clearly enough, history and hearsay have ostensibly shown us Keats himself. Yet when we look into his works we do not see a whole life "horribly clear," but rather spy another Keats lurking behind the black lattices of print. As we study his poems, he appears as a protean creature in a variety of ambiences. The ostensible and lurking Keats collaborated, each making a unique contribution, and, as we shall see, it was tragic when they clashed. They shared the same body, with its mortal ailments, as well as the same talents, the same loves, the same life circumstances. Yet each is distinguishable from the other by their unique reactions to the same happenings.

The ostensible Keats was a handsome, red-haired young man barely five feet tall, his gaze intense, his conversation witty. In his background was a big, rambling inn with abundant stables—the *Swan and Hoop*—in the northern outskirts of London. This establishment was kept by one John Jennings. His daughter Frances married her father's chief ostler, Thomas Keats, and on October 31, 1795 was delivered of a healthy male infant, John. Two years later George was born, two years later again, Thomas, and in 1803, Fanny. That same year, when John was eight, he and George were packed off to a boarding school at Enfield kept by the Reverend Clarke. It was not a prestigious institution such as Eton or Harrow, but from what we know of its scholars, the instruction was kind and thorough. A year afterwards John's father, although a skilled equestrian, was killed in a fall from his horse. John was fifteen in 1810 when his mother's tuberculosis became fatal. He, his brothers and Fanny were cared for by their widowed grandmother until her death in 1814, when Richard Abbey, a tea merchant, was appointed their financial guardian.

At sixteen John started to study medicine, which he continued until he was twenty-one years old, first apprenticed to a private practitioner and then attending lectures and demonstrations at two of the great London hospitals, Guy's and St. Thomas's. He endured listening to the screams of patients as they had their gangrenous limbs cut off, was humiliated by the futility of prescribing ineffective and nauseating pills and potions. He inhaled the odors of sickness—from pus, from excreta and from unwashed bodies. Finally, in 1816, the Society of Apothecaries gave him a license to practice the respectable and lucrative calling of medicine, but this Keats refused to do. His friend Charles Brown later wrote,

> He ascribed his inability to an overwrought apprehension of every possible chance of doing evil in the wrong direction of the instrument. 'My last operation,' he told me, 'was the opening of a man's temporal artery. I did it with the utmost nicety; but, reflecting on what passed through my mind at the time, my dexterity seemed a miracle, and I never took up the lancet again.'[2]

In the autumn of 1816 he told Charles Cowden Clarke, his erstwhile teacher, that he could no longer concentrate on his medical studies:

> The other day, for instance, during a lecture there came a sunbeam into the room, and with it a whole troop of creatures floating in the ray, and I was off with them to Oberon and fairyland.[3]

Despite Richard Abbey spluttering protests and insults, Keats insisted that he had the ability to support himself as a poet. However, financial need was not as compelling as his need to write. At this time Keats was chronically unhappy, and on a holiday in Margate reported to his brother George,

> Full many a dreary hour have I past,
> My brain bewilder'd, and my mind o'ercast
> With heaviness...[4]

Battling his low spirits, he wrote an ode to an epicene figure, Hope, whom he begged to dispel despair and despondency, to protect those whom he loved, to uphold the country's liberal politics, and continually to "wave...silver pinions" over his head.[5] He wrote a similar ode to Apollo, a little less melancholy, suggesting that he saw himself as a lonely outsider while the poets clustered around the "God of Song."[6] Yet these quasi-parental figures, Hope and Apollo, were not enough comfort. He identified himself with other poets on the basis of sorrow. There was Chatterton, a destitute adolescent who had committed suicide some 25 years before Keats was born, with whom he commisserated, "O Chatterton, how very sad thy fate!"[7] There was Lord Byron, whom he described as "sweetly sad" and begged him to "warble a tale of pleasing woe."[8]

A more effective method of overcoming melancholy is to attack. Here his political views were of assistance. Writing on peace in 1814 to celebrate the victory over France, Keats commanded the population of Europe to run their politics in a more effective fashion:

> ...let not scepter'd tyrants see
> That thou must shelter in thy former state;
> Keep thy chains burst, and boldly say thou art free;
> Give thy kings law—leave not uncurb'd the great...[9]

He was most annoyed by compatriots who had the termerity to celebrate the anniversary of Charles II's restoration: "Infatuate Britons," he called them. The most direct antagonism came in a sonnet on Leigh Hunt's liberation from prison. Leigh Hunt, a liberal editor and Keats' first publisher, had been incarcerated for "showing truth to flatter'd State"—in other words, insulting the Prince Regent. Keats jeered that he had not really been imprisoned, but rather gallivanted with Spenser and Milton. He ended with

> Who shall his fame impair
> When thou art dead and all thy wretched crew?[10]

These struggles to raise his spirits were unavailing, yet Keats saw possibilities of happiness if he could attain a new self image. Said he,

> But there are times, when those that love the bay,[11]
> Fly from all sorrowing, far, far away
> A sudden glow comes on them; naught they see
> In water, earth, or air, but poesy.[12]

3

In *Sleep and Poetry* he foresaw a glorious existence as a poet:

> O Poesy! for thee I grasp my pen
> That am not yet a glorious denizen
> Of thy wide heaven...
>
> ...imaginings will hover
> Round my fire-side, and haply there discover
> Vistas of solemn beauty...
>
> Then the events of this wide world I'd seize
> Like a strong giant, and my spirit teaze
> Till at its shoulders it should proudly see
> Wings to find out an immortality...
>
> O for ten years, that I may overwhelm
> Myself in poesy, so I may do the deed
> That my own soul has to itself decreed...

A successful, happy man lurked, waiting to be born. Keats wrote about this to his friend George Felton Mathew, evidently identifying with Mathew as he did so:

> For thou wast once a flowret blooming wild,
> Close to the source, bright, pure, and undefil'd,
> Whence gush the streams of song; in happy hour
> Came chaste Diana from her shady bower...
>
> Beheld thee, pluck'd thee, cast thee in a stream...
>
> How from a flower, into a fish of gold
> Apollo changed thee; how thou next didst seem
> A black-eyed swan upon the widening stream
> And when thou first didst in that mirror trace
> The placid features of a human face...[13]

The role of the lurking Keats entailed transforming distasteful memories into beautiful poetry. In these lines there is perhaps an association which Keats would not have faced knowingly—the memory of a pitiful little unborn infant still attached to the umbilical cord, floating in a jar of

4

preservative in a hospital museum. A universal symbol of birth is emergence from the water; the swan is seen in this way as it floats on the surface. This is particularly apt here, since the swan has always been an epithet for poets: Dr. Johnson called Shakespeare the Swan of Avon, and Virgil was the Swan of Mantua. When Keats wrote to Cowden Clarke of his intention to dedicate himself to verse, he modestly compared himself to a swan:

> Just like that bird am I in loss of time,
> Whene'er I venture on the stream of rhyme...

The same metaphor in the different setting appears in *Calidore—A Fragment,* written in 1817. Calidore paddled over a lake and was greeted on land by old and young people on horseback.[14] Keats may have vaguely remembered hearing of his own birth, when he was received by his grandparents as well as his parents, hence the two old and two young equestrians. Ruminating on his birth would have brought him to the memory of what he had heard of the courtship of his parents, which every child considers the epitome of romance. He was moved to "tell a tale of chivalry." The setting was Spenserian. A knight, well-equipped with phallic symbols—"large white plumes" and a lance pointed "slantingly"—meets

> ...some lady sweet,
> Who cannot feel for cold her tender feet,
> From the worn top of some old battlement
> Hails it with tears, her stout defender sent:
> And from her own pure self no joy dissembling,
> Wraps round her ample robe with happy trembling.

In Spenser's time, in Keats' time, and in our own, bare feet and an ample robe are bedroom garb. It would have been impossible for Keats to recognize what these lines referred to, so poignant and intimate were they. He could only speak freely if they were disguised. He also had reactions appropriate to one who would be a hidden witness to parental intimacy:

> ...I will follow with due reverence,
> And start with awe at mine own strange pretence.

These lines, called "Specimen of an Induction to a Poem," might more aptly be "An Induction of a Poet."

Another demonstration of how the lurking Keats came into being can be found in lines written in 1816. They start with the utmost reality:

I stoop tip-toe upon a little hill...said the ostensible Keats, possibly reacting involuntarily to his shortness. He delighted in what he experienced: "a little noiseless noise among the leaves"—"a bush of May flowers with the bees about them"—"a lush laburnum"—"a filbert hedge with wild briar overtwined/and clumps of woodbine taking the soft wind"—"the spreading bluebells"—"minnows." Yet he craved companionship:

> ...naught less sweet, might call my thoughts away,
> Than the soft rustle of a maiden's gown
> Fanning away the dandelion's down;
> Than the light music of her nimble toes
> Patting against the sorrel as she goes.
> How she would start, and blush, thus to be caught
> Playing in all her innocence of thought.
> O let me lead her gently o'er the brook,
> Watch her half-smiling lips, and downward look;
> O let me for one moment touch her wrist;
> Let me one moment to her breathing list;
> And as she leaves me may she often turn
> Her fair eyes looking through her locks auburne.

Here is a beautiful, congenial girl, auburn-haired like Keats himself, but he only wanted a few moments' dalliance. Then the lurking Keats took over:

> ...the mind may hover till it dozes
> Or which it well may take a pleasant sleep...

He turns to address the Moon:

> O Maker of sweet poets, dear delight
> Of this fair world, and all its gentle livers...
> Closer of lovely eyes to lovely dreams,
> Lover of loneliness, and wandering...

Queen of the wide air; Thou most lovely queen
Of all the brightness that mine eyes have seen!
As thou exceedest all things in thy shine,
So every tale, does this sweet tale of thine.
O for three words of honey, that I might
Tell but one wonder of thy bridal night!

The wonder is unexpected; it is a sickroom rather than a nuptial bed:

The breezes were ethereal, and pure,
And crept through half-closed lattices to cure
The languid sick; it cool'd their fever'd sleep,
And soothed them into slumbers full and deep.
Soon they awoke clear eyed; nor burnt with thirsting,
Nor with hot fingers, nor with temples bursting,
And springing up, they met the wond'ring sight
Of their dear friends, nigh foolish with delight;
Who feel their arms, and breasts, and kiss and stare,
And on their placid foreheads part the hair.

This scene is all too vivid, more deeply experienced even than the delights of the little hill. Keats had returned from school to care for his mother as she was dying of tuberculosis. How deep his wishes for her recovery must have been, the more that he had been stimulated by intimacy with the invalid, inappropriate for his age. How poignant to minister, often unavailingly, to her suffering. After he returned to boarding school, the end came, and Keats is said to have crawled underneath a desk to hide his tears from the other boys. A yearning for her revival and well-being became an inescapable part of the lurking Keats and a perpetual incentive for his creative life.

Footnotes to Chapter 1

1 *Letters of John Keats,* ed. Robert Gittings (London: Oxford University Press, 1970) p. 122 (hereafter cited as Gittings, *Letters*).

2 Robert Gittings, *John Keats,* (Boston: Little, Brown and Company, 1968.) p. 84. Brown was in error here. It was not the arteries that were lanced, but the veins.

3 Ibid, p.85

4 *To My Brother George*

5 *To Hope*

6 *Ode to Apollo*

7 Thomas Chatterton disclaimed his own poems and tried to pass them off as antiquities.

8 *To Byron*

9 *On Peace*

10 Actually, Leigh Hunt's fame was impaired when Charles Dickens caricatured him as Mr. Skimpole in *Bleak House.*

11 Short for the bay (laurel) wreath given to successful poets.

12 *To My Brother George*

13 *Epistle to George Felton Mathew*

14 He is named for one of Spenser's knights, but does not resemble him in any way, since the original Calidore was a belligerent character who conquered the "Blatant Beast" in *The Faerie Queene.*

Chapter II

Heaven lies about us in our infancy.
William Wordsworth
Intimations of Immortality

Over the entrance to the family coaching inn hung a sign that Keats must have seen every time he visited his grandparents. The sign showed that large white bird which later represented Keats as a poet; it showed something too that a child or a tipsy customer would call a hoop, but which looked like the full moon. This memory of the inn sign might have had no emotional significance to Keats, had it not been reinforced by his classical studies. As he explained to his young sister about his poetic romance, *Endymion:*

> Perhaps you might like to know what I am writing about. I will tell you.
>
> Many years ago there was a young handsome shepherd who fed his flocks on a mountain's side called Latmus—he was a very contemplative sort of person and lived solitary among the trees and plains little thinking that such a beautiful creature as the Moon was growing mad in love with him—however so it was; and when he was asleep on the grass, she used to come down from heaven and admire him excessively for a long time; and at last could not refrain from carrying him away in her arms to the top of that high mountain Latmus while he was a-dreaming—but I dare say you have read this and all the other beautiful tales which have come down from the ancient times of that beautiful Greece. If you have not let me know and I will tell you more at large of others quite as delightful.[1]

While a swan could symbolize a poet, a shepherd actually was a poet. Translations of pastoral verses by Theocritus, the heritage of Grecian Sicily, established the shepherd less as a custodian of livestock and more as a gracious wooer and conversationalist. Spenser also celebrated the poetic propensities of this calling in his volume *The Shep-*

herd's Calendar. "And every shepherd tells his tale/under the hawthorne in the dale," said Milton.[2]

While still upon the "little hill" the lurking Keats had pictured a union of the moon goddess—Cynthia or Diana—with a shepherd whom he called Endymion after the Greek myth. However, he apparently had been uncertain as to which generation Endymion belonged to —was he lover, child, or both?

> Cynthia! I cannot tell the greater blisses
> That followed thine, and thy dear shepherd's kisses:
> Was there a poet born?—but now no more,
> My wand'ring spirit must no further soar.

Nevertheless, his spirit wandered on, in the epic *Endymion,* for over 4000 rhymed iambic pentameters, during which he encountered not only his mother, but the other significant figures of his early years as well. His person was manly, but he was newborn—so his reactions were infantile. A baby is most acceptable to his elders when he sleeps, safe and making no demands. As we spy on the lurking Keats as Endymion, we see him ending passionate encounters and general festivities with a snooze or even a prolonged nap. He is the most somnolent character in English literature, including even the Fat Boy in Dickens' *Pickwick Papers.* Not that the lurking Keats saw Endymion as infantile—he had to be handsome and mature enough to charm the moon goddess down from the heavens. He is introduced in

> ...a fair-wrought car
> Easily rolling so as scarce to mar
> The freedom of three steeds of dapple brown:
> Who stood therein did seem of great renown
> Among the throng. His youth was fully blown,
> Showing like Ganymede to manhood grown
> And, for those simple times, his garments were
> A chieftain king's: beneath his breast, half bare,
> Was hung a silver bugle, and between
> His nervy knees there lay a boar-spear keen.[3]

The story begins with a gigantic celebration in honor of Pan. Endymion does not join in, but lingers with "shepherds gone in eld." The lurking Keats must have recalled those family gatherings where he had been confused and perhaps even frightened by the grownup hilarity and his grandparents had taken care of him. He fondly describes the revelers as "fair creatures, whose young children's children bred/Thermopylae its heroes." Amid the hurly-burly of gossiping elders, Endymion is "dead still as a marble man/frozen in that old tale Arabian." Peona arrives—his "sweet sister." But Keats' only sister was eight years his junior, and unlikely to have led him "like some midnight spirit-nurse," "guarding his forehead with her round elbow" and his slow footsteps from "stumbling over stumps." Her function was always to comfort. The name Peona, if derived from Paean, physician to the Gods, would be particularly appropriate to a woman who healed with love. Sometimes the figures in the epic are less identifiable as persons than they are as the roles and relationships that the young child had with them. For instance, at times Frances Keats, the mother, might have been replaced by a particularly kind and loveable nursemaid.

In a sequestered spot of Peona's choosing, Endymion dozes again, then wakes to tell her the source of his aloofness. He had fallen asleep among enchanted poppies, when the moon goddess came down and carried him away in her arms. Said he,

> I felt upmounted in that region
> Where falling stars dart their artillery forth...
>
> ...I was not fearful, nor alone,
> But lapp'd and lull'd along the dangerous sky.

The magic of the lurking Keats is shown in the way he could express the commonplaces of an infant's existence in these exquisite lines. The high point of this time of life is to be picked up, carried and fondled. But characteristically, he and the goddess fall asleep on a flowery hilltop, and when he awakes she has left him. A mood change occurs, brought about by something the lurking Keats would never have allowed in consciousness, but which remained potent all the same. Private memories of an infant or toddler—desires for intimacy, and secret self-stimulation—feel shameful in retrospect. Thus Endymion reacts when in his moon-goddess's absence he awakes:

> ...all the pleasant hues
> Of heaven and earth had faded: deepest shades
> Were deepest dungeons...

He remembers,

> ...if an innocent bird
> Before my heedless footsteps stirr'd, and stirr'd
> In little journeys, I beheld in it
> A disguised demon, missioned to knit
> My soul with utter darkness...

A small child left alone may feel abandoned, and unable to reach the beloved adult whose company he craves. Endymion, feeling helpless to find the goddess, loiters by forest pools, seeking her reflection, until he

> ...reach'd a splashing fountain's side
> ...near a cavern mouth...

> ...what gentle tongue,
> What whisperer disturb'd his gloomy rest?
> It was a nymph uprisen to the breast
> In the fountain's pebbly margin, and she stood
> 'Mong lillies, like the youngest of the brood.

She was not the goddess he sought. She says, "I am but as a child to gladden thee." A nymph, the youngest of the brood, sitting in a fountain, suggests baby sister Fanny in a washbasin. Her appearance in a fountain is also reminiscent of the way Keats described Mathew coming into the world out of the water. It is likely enough that Fanny's actual birth provoked eight-year-old brother John's curiosity as to whence she came. The answer was incredibly shocking; Fanny had come from inside Mama, and so had John and the other boys. Although terrified, the lurking Keats urged himself to explore his origin, with

> ...he ne'er is crown'd
> With immortality, who fears to follow
> Where airy voices lead: so through the hollow,
> The silent mysteries of earth, descend!

> ...he fled
> Into the fearful deep...

'Twas far too strange, and wonderful for sadness
Sharpening, by degrees, his appetite
To dive into the deepest.

What he found does not suggest a recollection of anatomical explorations from his hospital days, but rather reports of visits to Westminster Abbey or to the famous cavern known as Wookey Hole. A child, marveling at news of his prenatal existence, realizes that his siblings came from the same place. So Keats would have expected now to encounter his brother George, and accordingly, Endymion found Adonis asleep here. Suitably enough, Cybele, grandmother-goddess or midwife, passes by without lingering.

This return to his intrauterine existence did not give him the sought-for intimacy with the moon goddess. He had to go back to an even earlier time. So he said,

...when yet a child
I oft have dried my tears when thou hadst smiled.
Thou seem'dst my sister: hand in hand we went
From eve to morn across the firmament.

Keats' mother, the original of the moon goddess, actually was the sister of one Midgely John Jennings. If the lurking Keats now resented his goddess's actual brother, this would account for a diatribe which seems otherwise irrelevant:

...with not one tinge
Of sanctuary splendor, not a sight
Able to face an owl's, they still are dight
By the blear-eyed nations in empurpled vests,
And crowns, and turbans. With unladen breasts
Save of blown self-applause, they proudly mount
To their spirit's perch, their being's high account
Their tip-top nothings, their dull skies, their thrones...

Midgely John Jennings had enlisted as a seaman in the Royal Navy and been promoted to commissioned rank, an unusual achievement. It would have been likely enough for a small boy to resent the adulation given his uncle in his uniform when he came home on leave. Nor did the gallant sailor endear himself to his nephew grown older, for then he

13

was at odds with Keats' mother over their inheritance. So at this point the lurking Keats, as Endymion, finds Grandfather instead:

> He saw far in the concave green of the sea
> An old man sitting calm and peacefully.
> Upon a weeded rock this old man sat,
> And his white hair was awful, and a mat
> Of weeds were cold beneath his cold thin feet
> And, ample as the largest winding-sheet,
> A cloak of blue wrapp'd up his aged bones...

Grandpa evokes uncomplimentary memories of Grandma, when, inexorable for the protesting children's health, she distributed nauseating doses of medication—probably rhubarb and soda, brimstone and treacle. Grandpa, here named Glaucus, described her as Circe:

> Seated upon an uptorn forest root
> And all around her shapes, wizard and brute,
> Laughing and wailing, groveling...

> Avenging, slow,
> Anon she took a branch of mistletoe,
> And emptied on't a black dull-gurgling phial:
> Groan'd one and all, as if some piercing trial
> Was sharpening for their pitiable bones.
> She lifted up the charm: appealing groans
> From their poor breasts were sueing to her ear
> In vain; remorseless as an infant's bier
> She whisk'd against their eyes the sooty oil.
> Whereat was heard a noise of painful toil,
> Increasing gradual to a tempest rage,
> Shrieks, yells, and groans of torture-pilgrimage;
> Until their grieved bodies 'gan to bloat
> And puff from the tail's end to stifled throat...

Although Grandmother had made the boyhood Keats feel like a pitiful little monster and writhe with cathartics, Grandfather had undoubtedly told him that his was the mission to carry on the family line. The lurking Keats fancied himself resurrecting all those ancestral lovers now sleeping in West Country churchyards, although he pictured them as drowned:

> Such thousands of shut eyes in order plac'd;
> Such ranges of white feet, and patient lips
> All ruddy,—for here death no blossom nips.
> He mark'd their brows and foreheads; saw their hair
> Put sleekly to one side with nicest care
> And each one's gentle wrists, with reverence,
> Put cross-wise to his heart...

The drowned lovers revive, joyfully greet each other, and celebrate the family reunion. True to form, Endymion falls asleep. The greatgrandparents, brought back from the dead, did not mean as much as the lurking Keats had hoped. Instead, they reminded him that his mother was no glorious goddess, but a very unfortunate lady—arthritic, tubercular, widowed and then married to a disastrous second husband. He remembered longingly the old home, before he had gone off to boarding school:

> ...the spirit culls
> Unfaded amaranth when wild it strays,
> Through the old garden ground of boyish days.

Here his mother appears as a sorrowing stranger from India. With her Endymion falls in love, deserting the adored moon goddess. None of the other relationships he has tried have been successful. When he awoke from his nap among the enchanted poppies, his sojourn in the moon goddess's arms was tantalizingly short. His prenatal exploration left him lonely. His role as brother/rival was distasteful, and when he went further back in time he was caught up in one of those apparently unavoidable family parties. The only way he had not tried to approach his mother was as husband. Now for the Indian maid he offers to set up a minuscule sylvan housekeeping, such as he must have fancied before he left for boarding school at eight years of age:

> Where shall our dwelling be? Under the brow
> Of some steep mossy hill, where ivy dun
> Would hide us up, although spring leaves were none...
>
> O thou wouldst joy to live in such a place

> Dusk for our loves, yet light enough to grace
> Those gentle limbs on mossy bed reclin'd...
>
> Honey from out the gnarled hive I'll bring,
> And apples, warm with sweetness, gather thee...

And all the time the figure who represents the kind and nurturing mother, Peona, stands by. The lurking Keats admits that the dilemma drives Endymion mad:

> ...at this he press'd
> His hands against his face, and then did rest
> His head upon a mossy hillock green,
> And so remain'd as he a corpse had been...
>
> [he] tripp'd lightly on, in sort of deathful glee,
> Laughing at the clear stream and setting sun,
> As though they jests had been...

Said he,

> Why, I have been a butterfly, a lord
> Of flowers, garlands, love-knots, silly posies,
> Groves, meadows, melodies, and arbour roses
> My kingdom's at its death, and just it is
> That I should die with it...

The black hair of the bereaved Indian maid becomes the golden locks of the moon goddess, and after three kisses she and Endymion disappear. It could be death, but the lurking Keats made it glorious—a triumphant union of the Swan, himself, and the Hoop, his celestial mother.

Footnotes for Chapter II

1 Gittings, *Letters,* p. 18

2 *L'Allegro*

3 Here is authentic family tradition. The chariot with its three horses is hardly suitable for a shepherd in carrying out his occupation, but is reminiscent of the mounts and vehicles the gentry confided to the care of the livery stable at the Swan and Hoop.

Chapter III

The noble heart that harbors virtuous thought,
And is with child of glorious great intent,
Can never rest, until it forth has brought,
The eternal brood of glory excellent.
  Edmund Spenser
  The Faerie Queene

Such a revival of the past as the epic *Endymion* could only be achieved by denying the origins of its characters and happenings—otherwise the relevant memories would have been too painful to endure, too belittling to face. But had these memories not been cogent in Keats' life, they would not have given him the drive to accomplish all he did. In order to relive as Endymion the experiences of a beloved infant, the newborn lurking Keats needed the cooperation of his ostensible counterpart. He lured the ostensible Keats into this labor by two considerations. As he explained to his brother George,

> As to what you say about my being a poet, I can return no answer but by saying that the high idea I have of poetical fame makes me think I see it towering too high above me. At any rate, I have no right to talk until Endymion is finished. It will be a test, a trial of my powers of imagination, and chiefly of my invention, by which I must make 4000 lines of one bare circumstance and fill it with poetry. And when I consider that this is a great task and that one day it will take me but a dozen paces towards the temple of fame, it makes me say: God forbid that I should be without such a task.[1]

In another context, he declared,

> ,...a long poem is a test of invention which I take to be the polar star of poetry, as fancy is the sails and imagination the rudder. Did our great poets ever write short pieces, I mean in the shape of tales? That same invention seems indeed of late years to have been forgotten as a poetical excellence. But enough of this. I will

put on no laurels 'til I have finished Endymion.[2]

In 1817, while the lurking Keats as Endymion was luxuriating in some of the most beautiful scenes ever described, as for instance "a shady, fresh and ripply cove/where nested was an arbor"—"a dusky empire and its diadems/One faint eternal eventide of gems"—"sapphire columns, or fantastic bridge/Athwart a flood of crystal,"—the ostensible Keats, shaken and chilled, was rattling on top of coaches to the Isle of Wight, to Margate, to Canterbury, back to Hampstead, and on to Oxford. He described to Leigh Hunt the vicissitudes of these travels:

> I went to the Isle of Wight, thought so much about poetry so long together that I could not get to sleep at night; in a week or so I became not over-capable in my upper stories and set forth pell-mell for Margate, at least 150 miles, because, forsooth, I fancied that I should like my old lodging there and should contrive to do without trees. Another thing, I was too much in solitude, and consequently was obliged to be in continual burning of thought as an only resource.[3]

It had been hard work, pushing a quill pen over sheet after sheet of manuscript paper, finding comparisons and similes, choosing vivid words and painting verbal pictures, selecting the phrases and characters admired in the classics, reliving anguish now superceded, and all the time aware of the reviewers baring their teeth to attack his offspring.

His early poems had shown promise, particularly the sonnet which he wrote with great speed "before breakfast," after visiting Cowden Clarke and seeing a new acquisition—Chapman's translation of Homer:

> Much have I travell'd in the realms of gold,
> And many goodly states and kingdoms seen...

The sonnet reveals Keats' attachment to the classics, which would continue throughout his creative life:

> Then felt I like some watcher of the skies
> When a new planet swims into his ken;

Or like stout Cortez when with eagle eyes
He star'd at the Pacific—and all his men
Look'd at each other with a wild surmise—
Silent, upon a peak in Darien.[4]

However, his efforts had been published without much acclaim. Versifying could hardly yet be considered an adequate financial support. Although it was a reward in itself—the satisfaction of frustrated longings, new enjoyment of lost elusive gratifications—Keats was exhausting himself by reliving the first few years of his life in as many months.

At the same time, the ostensible Keats was harrassed by an apparent lack of funds. A substantial legacy left by his grandmother had been put in trust to Messrs. Abbey and Sandell without telling Keats about the extent of this resource. The trustees prudently withheld all they could, to encourage him to find another means of support—if not medicine, "hat-making."

Nevertheless, Keats was beginning to establish himself as a literary figure. Writing to Mathew, he said,

Sweet are the pleasures that to verse belong,
And doubly sweet a brotherhood in song...[5]

This brotherhood included poetasters such as Leigh Hunt; Benjamin Bailey, studying holy orders; John Hamilton Reynolds, an insurance broker; and James Rice and Richard Woodhouse, young barristers. They uplifted Keats by their enthusiasm and sympathy for his work, although they themselves rhymed and wrote in meter as their sisters did embroidery—to pass an idle hour by making something beautiful. Unlike the substantial impression we have of Keats, these characters appear as pencil sketches scribbled in the margins of texts.

Footnotes for Chapter III

1 Gittings; *Letters,* p. 26

2 Ibid, p. 27

3 Ibid, p. 9

4 *On First Looking Into Chapman's Homer*

5 *Epistle to George Felton Mathew*

Chapter IV

The child is father of the man.
William Wordsworth
My Heart Leaps Up

After *Endymion,* with its reliving of infantile relationships, the lurking Keats matured. This is shown by the attitudes towards his contemporaries expressed in his verses. At first he addressed the young women of suburban London as though they were nymphs and goddesses of the fantasied forests of ancient Greece. For instance, of one Mary Frogley, admired by George, he said

> Hadst thou liv'd in days of old,
> O what wonders had been told
> Of thy lively countenance...

He managed, though, in the present, to list her charms eloquently and all-inclusively. Then he asked Georgiana Augusta Wylie, whom George later married,

> In what diviner moments of the day
> Art thou most lovely?

Contemplating these fair nymphs, he found "light feet, dark violet eyes and parted hair/soft dimpled hands, white neck, and creamy breast" most alluring, and particularly adorable a personality "like a milk-white lamb that bleats for man's protection." He might have been a mere shepherd seeking acceptance from deities, so importunate was his tone. He tried to coax one of the Mathew girls with

> O come, dearest Emma...

He spared no compliments, calling her "beauteous Emma" and "lovely girl." When she and her sister gave him a shell as a souvenir of a seaside holiday, his thanks were effusive:

> If a cherub on pinions of silver descending

23

Had brought me a gem from the fretwork of heaven...

It had not created a warmer emotion
That the present, fair nymphs, I was bless'd with from you.

He even loved despite bad behavior:

Woman! when I behold thee, flippant, vain,
Inconstant, childish, proud and full of fancies;
Without that modest softening that enhances
The downcast eye, repentant of the pain
That its mild light creates to heal again:
E'en then, elate, my spirit leaps, and prances,
E'en then my soul with exultation dances...

For that to love, so long, I've dormant lain...

He did not blame the nymphs for their indifference. It was his fault for being so short. He said to Mary Frogley,

Had I a man's fair form, then might my sighs
Be echoed swiftly through that ivory shell
Thine ear...

But ah! I am no knight whose foeman dies...

In 1814, still an apothecary in outlook, he begged someone to

Fill for me a brimming bowl
And let me in it drown my soul:
But put some drug therein, designed
To banish Women from my mind...

This was the outcome of an encounter with a stranger in Vauxhall Gardens, the amusement park:

...the fairest form
That e'er my reveling eyes beheld,
That e'er my wandering fancy spell'd
In vain! Away I cannot chase

24

The melting softness of that face...

> My sight will never more be blest
> For all I see has lost its zest...

He admitted that he was responsible for his lack of success:

> Had she but known how beat my heart,
> And with one smile reliev'd its smart,
> I should have felt a sweet relief...

Evidently he had been too timid to make advances. Another poem written at this time represents youthful assertion made to cover actual diffidence:

> Give me women, wine and snuff
> Until I cry out "hold, enough!"
> You may do so sans objection
> Till the day of resurrection
> For bless my beard they aye shall be
> My beloved Trinity.

Verse by verse, the lurking Keats matured to discard the self-image and attitudes of babyhood for those of a virile youth. He celebrated a satisfactory encounter with,

> Unfelt, unheard, unseen,
> I've left my little queen...

He was explicit in January 1818, when recalling the prelude to a dalliance, he exclaimed,

> O blush not so! O blush not so!
> Or I shall think you knowing;
> And if you smile the blushing while,
> Then maidenheads are going.

A visit to Teignmouth was marked by amorous romps in the neighborhood with Devonshire dairymaids, which he remembered in

Where be ye going, you Devon maid?
And what have ye there in the basket?

I'll put your basket all safe in a nook,
Your shawl I hang up on the willow,
And we will sigh in the daisy's eye
And kiss on a grass green pillow.

He told his friend James Rice of a successful seduction:

Over the hill and over the dale
And over the Bourne to Dawlish,
Where Gingerbread wives have a scanty sale
And gingerbread nuts are smallish.

Rantipole Betty, she ran down a hill
And kicked up her petticoats fairly,
Says I "I'll be Jack if you will be Jill,"
So she sat on the grass debonnairly.

Here's somebody coming, here's somebody coming—
Says I, "Tis the wind at a parley,"
So without any fuss, any hawing and humming,
She lay on the grass debonnairly.

In time admiration gave way to sophisticated appraisals:

O! were I one of the Olympian twelve,
Their godships should pass this into a law,—
That when a man doth set himself in toil
After some beauty veiled far away,
Each step he took should make his lady's hand
More soft, more white, and her fair cheek more fair...

He boasts, in *Daisy's Song,* of being bolder than before:

The sun, with his great eye,
Sees not so much as I...

And O the spring—the spring!

I lead the life of a king!
Couch'd in the teeming grass,
I spy each pretty lass.

I look where no one dares,
And I stare where no one stares...

At another time, he expressed disillusionment:

O, I am frighten'd with most hateful thoughts!
Perhaps her voice is not a nightingale's,
Perhaps her teeth are not the fairest pearl...

and disparaged marriage in *Folly's Song:*

When wedding fiddles are a-playing
Huzza for folly O!

He hinted at seduction, describing how

A stranger lighted from his steed,
And ere he spake a word,
He seiz'd my lady's lilly hand,
And kiss'd it all unheard...

He kissed my lady's cherry lips
And kiss'd them all unheard...

The stranger walked into the bower,—
But my lady first did go,—
Aye hand in hand into the bower,
Where my lord's roses blow...

Two poems are graceful withdrawals from erotic relationships. In one
he tried to extricate himself from one of the Reynolds girls with

Think not of it, sweet one, so;-
Give it not a tear;
Sigh thou mayst, and bid it go
Any, any where.

Yet—as all things mourn awhile
At fleeting blisses,
Let us too! but be our dirge
A dirge of kisses.

He looked back on earlier dalliance with

In a drear-nighted December
Too happy, happy tree,
Thy brances ne'er remember
Their green felicity...

Ah! would 'twere so with many
A gentle girl and boy!
But were there ever any
Writh'd not at passed joy?
To know the change and feel it,
When there is none to heal it,
Nor numbed sense to steel it,
Was never said in rhyme.

In a corresponding fashion, Keats changed his attitude towards
other men. His first poems were affectionate epistles such as that to
Cowden Clarke, when he almost apologized for his audacity at becoming a poet, and ended with,

By this, friend Charles, you may full plainly see
Why I have never penn'd a line to thee:
Because my thoughts were never free, and clear,
And little fit to please a classic ear...

While enjoying the beauty of a holiday at Margate, he wrote to his brother George, ending

But what, without the social thought of thee
Would be the wonders of the sky and sea?

Keats dedicated his first verses to Leigh Hunt, who published them, with

In a time when under pleasant trees
Pan is no longer sought, I feel a free,
A leafy luxury, seeing I could please
With these poor offerings, a man like thee.

Writing to his friend Benjamin Haydon, painter of elaborate crowd scenes, Keats said,

> My feelings entirely fall in with yours...the idea of sending it
> [one of his sonnets] to Wordsworth put me out of breath—you
> know with what Reverence I would send my Wellwishes to him
> ...[1]

About Haydon, Wordsworth and Hunt, he had written,

> Great Spirits now on Earth are sojourning...

The Brotherhood of Song not only included his actual friends, but also bygone poets. As he said,

> How many bards gild the lapses of time!
> A few of them have ever been the food
> Of my delighted fancy...

His attitude toward Milton was ecstatically respectful. When he was shown a lock of Milton's hair, he showered him with admiring epithets:

> Chief of organic numbers!
> Old Scholar of the Spheres!
> Thy spirit never slumbers,
> But rolls about our ears,
> For ever, and for ever!

A sonnet to Kosciusko, the Polish patriot, expressed the same sentiments:

> Good Kosciusko, thy great name alone
> Is a full harvest whence to reap high feeling;
> It comes upon us like the glorious pealing
> Of the wide spheres...

Now unwittingly Keats had come to the stage where competitiveness supplants hero worship. On two occasions at least he contradicted what Reynolds wrote. Reynolds delighted in the persistence of Sherwood Forest, and Keats rebutted him with an emphatic

> No! those days are gone away...

in a sonnet to back up his views. Reynolds, courting a brunette, wrote that

> Dark eyes are dearer far
> Than those that mock the hyacinthine bell.

which led Keats to compose a sonnet extolling all kinds of blueness, especially in eyes. In a somewhat derogatory way, he copied Milton's *Il Pensoroso* and *L'Allegro,* combining two contrasts in one poem:

> Welcome joy and welcome sorrow,
> Lethe's weed and Hermes' feather...

He also joined Shelley and Hunt in writing competing sonnets about the Nile. The ostensible Keats was encouraged enough to persevere with his literary career, which matched the lurking Keats' increased social self-assurance.

Another characteristic of the age to which the lurking Keats had come was that of constructiveness. The adolescent boy is no longer interested in playthings and not yet ready for adult undertakings. He has no opportunity to build great edifices, except in fancy. Keats imagined two living places. Sitting on the shore at Teignmouth, he pictured a painting by Claude called *The Enchanted Castle.* He described it to Reynolds in a letter:

> A mossy place, a Merlin's Hall, a dream...

> Part of the building was a chosen See,
> Built by a banish'd Santon of Chaldee;
> The other part, two thousand years from him,
> Was built by Cuthbert de Saint Aldebrim
> Then there's a little wing, far from the Sun,
> Built by a Lapland Witch turn'd maudlin Nun;

And many other juts of aged stone
Founded with many a mason-devil's groan...

The doors all look as if they op'd themselves,
The windows as if latched by Fays and Elves...[2]

Back in Well Walk, in Hampstead, shunning the noisy and noisome children of his landlord, Keats castigated the vulgarity of the great vegetable market, Covent Garden, as a "monstrous beast" and a "promenade for cooks and ancient ladies." Instead he conjured up

...my room,—I'll have it in the pink;
It should be rich and sombre...

He went on, perhaps in a satiric vein, to list four large windows, golden vases, Turkish carpets, orange trees on the terrace outside,

A gorgeous room, but somewhat sad,
The draperies are so, as tho' they had
Been made for Cleopatra's winding-sheet...[3]

The jumble of objects of art suggests Hogarth's pictures of high life. How different from the simple home Endymion had pictured "under the brow of some steep mossy hill." It typifies the contrast between the infant-homebody and the young man-about-town that the lurking Keats had now become.

Footnotes for Chapter IV

1 *The Letters of John Keats,* ed. Maurice Buxton Forman (London: Oxford University Press, 1947) p. 11, (hereafter cited as Forman, *The Letters*).

2 *Epistle to John Hamilton Reynolds*

3 *The Castle Builder*

Chapter V

The pang of all the partings gone
And partings yet to be.
                    Francis Thompson
                    Daisy

Though the term "man-about-town" often implies that acquaintances and friends are all-important, this does not apply to Keats, who we know valued his brothers' company above all others. As he told Bailey,

> My love for my Brothers from the early loss or our parents and
> even for earlier misfortunes has grown into an affection 'passing
> the love of Women'[1]

A sonnet written on November 18, 1816 tell us

> Small, busy flames play through the fresh laid coals,
> And their faint cracklings o'er our silence creep
> Like whispers of the household gods that keep
> A gentle empire o'er fraternal souls.
> And while, for rhymes, I search around the poles,
> Your eyes are fixed, as in poetic sleep,
> Upon the lore so voluble and deep,
> That aye at fall of night our care condoles.
> This is your birth-day, Tom, and I rejoice
> That thus it passes smoothly, quietly.
> Many such eves of gently whisp'ring noise
> May we together pass...

When Tom began to cough and shiver with fever, showing symptoms all too reminiscent of their mother's last illness, the boys moved out to the cleaner air of Hampstead, on the high ground north of London. Unselfishly George undertook the longer daily round trip to his job in the city. But Tom continued to fail, and John took him to Teignmouth on the Devon shore for the sea breezes then considered a panacea.

At this time a significant event in Keats' family demonstrated emphatically the difference between his ostensible and lurking counterparts. George was about to marry Georgiana Wylie and planned to take her to homestead in the United States. Consciously, Keats was hardly able to handle his feelings about this parting, so he pretended he did not have them. A few weeks before George and Georgiana were to depart, Keats wrote to Bailey,

> This for many reasons has met with my entire consent...he will marry before he sets sail a Young Lady...of a nature liberal and high-spirited enough to follow him to the Banks of the Mississippi.

> I have this morning such a Lethargy that I cannot write...I am now so depressed that I have not an idea to put to paper—my hand feels like lead—I know very well 'tis all nonsense. In a short time I hope I shall be in a temper to feel sensibly your mention of my Book...I feel no spur at my Brother's going to America, and am almost stony-hearted about his wedding.[2]

Months later, Keats wrote to George and Georgiana in America,

> If you were here, my dear sister, I could not pronounce the words which I can write to you from a distance. I have a tenderness for you, and an admiration which I feel to be as great and more chaste than I can have for any woman in the world...

and went on to tell George,

> I have never made any acquaintance of my own, nearly all through your medium, my dear brother. Through you I know not only a sister but a glorious human being.[3]

An acrostic on Georgiana's married name was a further celebration of their new relationship.

The ostensible Keats had agreed with Reynolds to versify a 17th century translation of Boccaccio's *Decameron*. It was the lurking Keats who chose, from a wide variety of stories, one not only tragic but gruesome as well. The heroine, Isabella, lived in Florence, and was the sister of two avaricious, unscrupulous international merchants. Though wealthy, they were ambitious to become even richer by marrying Isabella to "some high noble and his olive-trees." This did not suit her; her love was for one of their employees, Lorenzo. Learning this, the brothers lured Lorenzo into the woods, murdered him, and buried his body:

> They told their sister how, with sudden speed,
> Lorenzo had ta'en ship for foreign lands...
>
> And she had died in drowsy ignorance,
> But for a thing more deadly dark than all...
>
> It was a vision.—in the drowsy gloom,
> The dull of midnight, at her couch's foot,
> Lorenzo stood, and wept...

The ghost described the place where he was buried. Next morning off she went, with the inevitable aged female companion. She found, she exposed the corpse of her dead lover, she dug it up. She caressed it, and, most macabre, she cut off the head, the head she loved so well, wrapped it in a scarf and buried it in a flower pot under a plant of sweet basil. Her tearful preoccupation with the plant aroused her brothers' suspicion:

> Yet they contrived to steal the Basil-pot,
> And to examine it in secret place
> The thing was vile with green and livid spot,
> And yet they knew it was Lorenzo's face:
> The guerdon of their murder they had got,
> And so left Florence in a moment's space,
> Never to turn again.—Away they went,
> With blood upon their heads, to banishment.
>
> And so she pined, and so she died forlorn...
>
> Still is the burthen sung—"O cruelty,
> "To steal my Basil-pot away from me!"

What pathos in this tale, beautifully told, of crime, death and insanity. And lurking beneath the pathos, what gratifying denial of present unhappiness. If two brothers are to be lost from sight, better banish them as murderers than have poor Tom die and George become a far-flung emigrant. And if Georgiana, his new-found sister, could only stay

35

home, ever more intent on the brother-in-law she loved, how much better than embarking from Liverpool.

The dreamer is always the hero of the dream—the poet is his own chief character. Willingly the lurking Keats undertook the remaining role, that of Lorenzo. The unhappy fact that he was killed and decapitated was nullified by his having an active and effective ghost. The lurking Keats could not recognize the possibility of his own non-existence. The reward of dying was the devotion that Isabella showered on that part of Lorenzo that remained to her—just as Cynthia had doted on the sleeping Endymion.

Why should Keats have imagined paying so heavy a price for a woman's affection, just when his own amorous adventures were prospering? The answer is that she whom he loved was the one living woman forbidden to him. Two years before, when he had written poems to Georgiana, her charms had so bewildered him that he had said,

> But thou to please wert nurtured so completely,
> That I can never tell which mood is best.

The fate of the lurking Keats as Lorenzo would exonerate him from any unacknowledged guilt he had for envy of George.

Consciously to correlate this ancient tale with the present parting would have been shocking. His ostensible reaction to the emigration of George and Georgiana was shorter:

> Sweet, sweet is the greeting of eyes,
> And sweet is the voice in its greeting...
>
> When adieus have grown old, and good-byes
> Fade away where old time is retreating.
>
> Warm the nerve of a welcoming hand,
> And earnest a kiss on the brow,
> When we meet over sea and o'er land
> Where furrows are new to the plough.

This prophecy was not to be fulfilled; Keats never saw Georgiana again.

Footnotes for Chapter V

1 Gittings, *Letters,* p. 99
2 Ibid., p. 97
3 Ibid., p. 159

Chapter VI

O Caledonia! stern and wild,
Meet nurse for a poetic child!
Sir Walter Scott
The Lay of the Last Minstrel

On June 22, 1818 the Liverpool coach from a London inn had as a passenger that 20-year-old girl whom Keats had called "nymph of the downward smile and sidelong glance." She was appraised by one of his friends as "not strictly handsome" but rather as "original" and having an "imaginative cast about her."[1] She was on her honeymoon with her beloved groom, George Keats. They were buoyed by hopes of a fortune to be made in an independent life in America.

A comparative stranger to his companions in the coach was a heavily built, prematurely bald, bespectacled man of thirty, Charles Brown, probably speaking with a Scots burr. Though a one-time merchant in Russia, and a playwright whose works were performed in Drury Lane, his moderate but adequate income was inherited rather than earned. Every summer, as now, he rented out his half-house in Wentworth Place on the edge of Hampstead Heath, and made an economical walking tour in his "ain country." For the last few months he and John Keats had found each other congenial company. He had invited Keats to join him, and by traveling together now, Keats was able to accompany George and Georgiana until they embarked from Liverpool. It was Keats' presence that made the trip a historic event. He was able to be there because of a happy discovery of unexpected funds, and because it was considered that he could discard his recent heavy responsibilities. Poor tubercular Tom was thought improved enough to exchange a brother's solicitude and the sea air at Teignmouth for the ministrations of Mrs. Bentley, their landlady, at Well Walk. Keats had had doubts about leaving Tom. He had misgivings about his own health as well, but optimism and the need to see distant scenes prevailed. The grandeur of the Highlands would be more inspiring than the humdrum glades and streams of Hampstead Heath. He equipped himself with four tiny volumes of Cary's translation of Dante's *Inferno* for mental sustenance

The coach travelers parted at Liverpool. John Keats and Brown went north, George and Georgiana sailed west.

The ostensible Keats was so solicitous of his young sister Fanny, captive of their guardian Abbey, and of weak and fevered Tom, that he painstakingly shared with them his impressions and emotions. He wrote to Tom,

> Descriptions are bad at all times. I did not intend to give you any, but how can I help it?[2]

Luckily, his letters from Scotland have been treasured since then, and even now we can stand beside him as he notes, foot by foot, the Ambleside waterfall:

> ...the waterfall itself, which I came suddenly upon, gave me a pleasant twinge. First we stood a little below the head about half way down the first fall, buried deep in trees, and saw it streaming down two more descents to the depth of nearly fifty feet—then we went on a jut of rock nearly level with the second fall-head, where the first fall was above us, and the third below our feet still —at the same time we saw that the water was divided by a sort of cataract island on whose other side burst out a glorious stream—then the thunder and the freshness. At the same time the different falls have as different characters; the first darting down the slate-rock like an arrow; the second spreading out like a fan—the third dashed into a mist...What astonishes me more than anything is the tone, the coloring...or, if I may so say, the intellect, the countenance of such places...I shall learn poetry here...[3]

We follow him along the western coast, with Ailsa Rock in view:

> When we left Cairn our road lay half way up the sides of a green mountainous shore, full of clefts of verdure and eternally varying —sometimes up sometimes down, and over little bridges going across green chasms of moss rock and trees—winding about every where. After two or three miles of this we turned suddenly into a magnificent glen finely wooded in parts—seven miles long—with a mountain stream winding down the midst— full of cottages in the most happy situations—the sides of the hills covered with sheep...At the end we had a gradual ascent and got among the tops of the mountains whence in a little time I

descried in the sea Ailsa Rock 940 feet height—it was 15 miles distant and seemed close upon us—the effect of Ailsa with the peculiar perspective of the Sea in connection with the ground we stood on, and the misty rain then falling gave me a complete idea of a deluge.[4]

With him we gaze about Loch Lomond:

...the water was a fine blue silvered and the mountains a dark purple the sun setting aslant behind them...[5]

Scenes were pleasing, but for the most part, people were not. The exception was a dancing class in Ireby, in Cumberland:

It was indeed "no new cotillion fresh from France." No, they kickit and jumpit with mettle extraordinary, and whiskit, and friskit, and toed it, and go'd it, and twirl'd it, and wheel'd it, and stamped it, and sweated it, tatooing the floor like mad; the difference between our country dances and these Scottish figures is about the same as leisurely stirring a cup o' tea and beating up a batter-pudding...I hope I shall not return without having got the Highland fling. There was as fine a row of boys and girls as you ever saw; some beautiful faces, and one exquisite mouth. I never felt so near the glory of Patriotism, the glory of making by any means a country happier. This is what I like better than scenery. I fear our continued moving from place to place, will prevent our becoming learned in village affairs; we are mere creatures of Rivers, Lakes and Mountains.[6]

Keats and Brown made their way through Lancashire, where they were confronted by the beginnings of the Industrial Revolution. Keats found the endless clatter of the spinning spindles distressing, and eagerly they continued on through the beauties of the Lake Country and over the Scottish border. Keats, who had admired the light feet of fair nymphs in Hampstead, took particular note of the barefoot women, ankle-deep in mud, who carried their shoes and stockings. Individuals he described with loathing; the custodian of Burns' cottage was

...a mahogany-faced old Jackass who knew Burns—he ought to have been kicked for having spoken to him.[7]

41

A quick side trip to Ireland evoked the following:

> On our return from Belfast we met...the Duchess of Dunghill...
> Imagine the worst dog kennel you ever saw placed upon two
> poles from a mouldy fencing. In such a wretched thing sat a
> squalid old Woman squat like an ape half starved from a scarcity
> of Buiscuit in its passage from Madagascar to the cape,—with a
> pipe in her mouth and looking out with a round-eyed skinny
> lidded inanity—with a sort of horizontal idiotic movement of her
> head...[8]

In a letter to Tom he made his feelings about the Scotch and the Irish
plain:

> A Scotchman will go wisely about to deceive you, an Irishman
> cunningly. An Irishman would bluster out of any discovery to his
> disadvantage...[9]

Keats' disparagement of those he met would seem to have arisen from
a denial of fatigue and discomfort. True, he wrote to Bailey that they
"bore the fatigue very well, twenty miles a day in general," and to
cheer George he said,

> I have had great confidence in your being well able to support the
> fatigue of your Journey since I have felt how much new Objects
> contribute to keep off a sense of ennui and fatigue; 14 miles here
> is not so much as the 4 from Hampstead to London.[10]

He could ignore the tax on his energy, but had to acknowledge cold—a
condition he hated. The low temperature spoiled his sojourn at the
goal of his trip, the tomb of Burns, and even inspired a sonnet:

> The short-liv'd, paly Summer is but won
> From Winter's ague, for one hour's gleam;
> Though sapphire-warm, their stars do never beam:
> All is cold beauty; pain is never done...[11]

As was to be expected in Scotland, downpours were frequent. These
hardly seemed to deter the walkers. One day they trudged fifteen
miles in the rain. Nor was there much respite when they remained in

shelter. There were few inns, and those inferior. Had there been better, they could not have afforded them. They availed themselves of the hospitality of hovels, which meant lying on dirt floors enveloped in smoke whose only escape was an open door. Worst of all was the food. The staple of the Highlands was a cake made of oats, insipid of taste and scratchy in the mouth. Keats had caught cold and his throat was sore. It was torture to swallow these. The sting of raw whiskey was another affliction, and the only respite was the bland monotony of eggs.

The ostensible Keats evidently bore patiently the hardships of the expedition, which increased as he used up his strength and his cold became worse, The lurking Keats was more active. He identified with personalities who could find some comfort in situations which were a hardship to him. One such occasion was a tramp through Kirk Cudbright County—"very beautiful, very wild." Brown entertained him by telling the story of Sir Walter Scott's recently published novel, *Guy Mannering*. A key character in this work is Meg Merrilies, of whom Keats said,

> Old Meg she was a Gipsey,
> And liv'd upon the Moors:
> Her bed it was the brown heath turf,
> And her house was out of doors.
>
> Her brothers were the craggy hills,
> Her sisters larchen trees—
> Alone with her great family,
> She liv'd as she did please.[12]

He commented to Tom,

> This morning we passed through some parts exactly suited to her.[13]

The reason for his choice could well be that here Meg was entirely at home and among her "sisters and brothers" nearby. Keats, on the other hand, was bereft of his family and feeling tired, cold, and hungry. Similarly, when after an arduous expedition by land and sea the travelers arrived at the island of Staffa, the ostensible Keats told Tom all about it:

One may compare the surface of the Island to a roof—this roof is supported by grand pillars of basalt standing together as thick as honeycombs. The finest thing is Fingal's Cave—it is entirely a hollowing out of Basalt Pillars. Suppose now the Giants who rebelled against Jove had taken a whole mass of black columns and bound them together like bunches of matches—and then with immense axes had made a cavern in the body of these columns …the roof is arched somewhat gothic wise and the length of some of the entire side pillars is 50 feet—About the island you might seat an army of Men each on a pillar. The length of the cave is 120 feet and from its extremity the view into the sea through the large Arch at the entrance…for solemnity and grandeur it far surpassed the finest Cathedral…[14]

As he struggled to do justice to these wonders, the lurking Keats intruded with,

Lo! I saw one sleeping there,
On the marble cold and bare.
While the surges wash'd his feet,
And his garments white did beat,
Drench'd about the sombre rocks…

"I am Lycidas," said he…

Anyone who could rest so pleasantly in the surf was surely to be envied. Lycidas could well have been in Keats' mind, since this was the name by which Milton eulogized his fellow student Edward King, drowned in these same waters.

Though the ostensible Keats was courageous and the lurking Keats ingenious in battling physical difficulties, debility was real and undeniable. After visiting Burns' cottage, he wrote lines so long the convey the sense of weariness:

There is charm in footing slow across a silent plain…
…room is there for a prayer,
That man may never lose his mind on mountains bleak
    and bare;
That he may stray league after league some great
    birthplace to find

44

And keep his vision clear from speck, his inward
    sight unblind.

Keats consulted a physician at Inverness, who ordered an immediate return home. He sailed in a boat from Cromarty—no pleasure trip, but less arduous than the same distance by road. Homecoming was no solace.

Tom was dying.

Footnotes for Chapter VI

1 Gittings, *John Keats,* p. 219

2 Gittings, *Letters,* p. 103

3 Ibid., p. 102

4 Ibid., p. 125

5 Ibid., p. 129

6 Ibid., p. 108

7 Ibid., p. 122

8 Ibid., p. 120

9 Ibid., p. 127

10 Ibid., p. 104

11 *On Visiting the Tomb of Burns*

12 Gittings, *Letters,* p. 111

13 Ibid., p. 116

14 Ibid., p. 142

Chapter VII

How are the mighty fallen.
2 Samuel I

Home again, life was nearly as strenuous as it had been in Scotland. Keats no longer trudged twenty miles a day deliberately, but fetching and carrying, feeding and bedmaking for weak and fevered Tom was continuous hard work. True, now food was better than the oat cakes which Keats had called "cursed," but with a sore throat and toothache his meals were endured rather than enjoyed. Besides physical efforts, there was the demand—to him urgent—that he justify himself as a poet. He had apologized for *Endymion* in its preface:

> The imagination of a boy is healthy, and the mature imagination of a man is healthy; but there is a space of life between, in which the soul is in a ferment, the character undecided, the way of life uncertain, the ambition thick-sighted; thence proceeds mawkishness, and all the thousand bitters which those men I speak of must necessarily taste in going over the following pages.

> I hope I have not in too late a day touched the beautiful mythology of Greece, and dulled its brightness: for I wish to try once more, before I bid it farewell.

When, for Haydon, he contemplated his next epic, it was with

> The nature of *Hyperion* will lead me to treat it in a more naked and Grecian manner, and the march of passion and endeavour will be undeviating. Apollo in *Hyperion*, being a far-seeing god, will shape his actions like one.[1]

For this undertaking he had harvested materials: what he saw in Scotland—the majesty of streams and mountains— and what he had read in the miniature volumes of Cary's Dante, carried in his knapsack.

But actual inspiration came from the stage at which the lurking Keats had arrived. After *Endymion* he had stopped toddling, had

47

strode as a schoolboy, endured hardships as an explorer. While on the "little hill" he had pictured the meeting of the shepherd and the moon goddess, and had asked "was there a poet born?" as though he saw himself as both mate and offspring. Now, by his conduct in *Hyperion* the generations are again confused. His theme was the overthrow of the primeval authorities such as Saturn and Hyperion by young deities such as Apollo. The "march of passion and endeavour" was far from undeviating. He started the narrative,

> Deep in the shady sadness of a vale,
> Far sunken from the healthy breath of morn...

where sat

> ...gray-hair'd Saturn, quiet as a stone...

Both by similarity and by contrast, the story is reminiscent of *Endymion*. Both begin with the leading character aloof, Endymion from reveling shepherds, Saturn from his tortured captive peers and followers. Both Saturn and Endymion are aroused and led off by nurturing females, and in the same way. With Endymion, Peona was "guarding his forehead with her round elbow/from low grown branches, and his footsteps slow/from stumbling over stumps," while with Saturn, Thea went "with backward footing through the shade a space:/He follow'd, and she turn'd to lead the way/Through aged boughs, that yielded like the mist..." Saturn is passive, his old right hand is "nerveless, listless, dead"—Endymion merely drowsy, though healthy. Here are no jubilant shepherds in the background, but grieving Titans:

> Meanwhile in other realms big tears were shed...
>
> The Titans, fierce, self-hid, or prison-bound
> Groan'd for the old allegiance once more,
> And listen'd in sharp pain for Saturn's voice.

There follows a debate; on one side the Titans who wish to defy the gods who conquered them, typically, Enceladus, exhorted:

> Speak! roar! shout! yell! ye sleepy Titans all.

His opponent, Oceanus, tries to comfort the Titans and make their defeat seem inevitable, even in a sense desirable:

> We fall by course of Nature's law, not
> Force of thunder...
>
> ...on our heels a fresh perfection treads,
> A power more strong in beauty, born of us
> And fated to excel us, as we pass
> In glory that old Darkness...

Clymene, Oceanus's daughter, testifies to hearing

> "A voice came sweeter, sweeter than all tune,
> "And still it cried, "Apollo! young Apollo!
> "The morning-bright Apollo! young Apollo!"

Having introduced the usurping sun-god, Keats turned to his precursor:

> But one of the whole mammoth-brood still kept
> His sov'reignty, and rule, and majesty—
> Blazing Hyperion on his orbed fire
> Still sat...
>
> But horrors portion'd to a giant nerve,
> Oft made Hyperion ache...
>
> Instead of sweets, his ample palate took
> Savour of poisonous brass and metal sick...

What Hyperion encountered was as loathsome as what he felt:

> "O spectres busy in a cold, cold gloom!
> "O lank-ear'd Phantoms of black-weeded pools!...
> So at Hyperion's words, the Phantoms pale
> Bestirr'd themselves, thrice horrible and cold;
> And from the mirror'd level where he stood
> A mist arose, as from a scummy marsh.

> At this, through all his bulk an agony
> Crept gradual, from the feet unto the crown...

The first two books of the epic are summed up with,

> ...in alternate uproar and sad peace,
> Amazed were those Titans utterly.

With little introduction, the third book shows "Apollo is once more the golden theme." The place is the island of Delos,

> ...with thine olives green,
> And poplars, and lawn-shading palms, and beech...

Apollo leaves his mother and twin sister to greet the "awful goddess" Mnemosyne, mother of the Muses, presiding over memory and knowledge. She had brought Apollo a lyre, thus potentially making him a poet. Here Keats correlates being a poet with being Apollo, saying, "Knowledge enormous makes a God of me." He had implied the same identification in his poem *Apollo and the Graces,* when the Graces all clamored to go with him. Becoming a God was no easy accomplishment:

> ...with a pang
> As hot as death's is chill, with fierce convulse
> Die into life; so young Apollo anguish'd...
> Apollo shrieked—and lo! from all his limbs
> Celestial

Here the poem stops in mid-line. Keats has said all he has to say, or dreaded further elaborations.

How difficult to tell what the lurking Keats is up to! He might well be one of the defeated Titans, having known discomfort in Scottish hovels which resembled their lot. The lines

> Instead of thrones, hard flint they sat upon,
> Couches of rugged stone, and slaty ridge...

recall how delighted Keats was to find himself once more in an uphol-stered chair after his trip.[2] Hyperion's "savor of poisonous brass and metal sick" could well match the perpetually nauseating taste of pus

50

from Keats' ulcerated pharynx. Yet there is indication that Keats saw the Titans as the primeval movers of his long-gone infancy. He keeps referring to their gigantic size. They are a "mammoth brood," Saturn's footprints are "large along the margin-sand." As for Thea,

> By her in stature the tall Amazon
> Had stood a pigmy's height...
>
> Her face was large as that of Memphian sphinx...

We know that he was sensitive about his own shortness, but this goes further. This enormousness is how grownups appear to the baby on the floor. At first they seem like Gods. Coelus says to Hyperion that the Titans were

> ...divine
> In sad demeanor, solemn, undisturb'd,
> Unruffled, like high Gods, ye lived and ruled...

Then disillusionment sets in:

> Now I behold in you fear, hope, and wrath,
> Actions of rage and passion...
>
> Sad sign of ruin, sudden dismay, and fall!

Except for Saturn and Hyperion, the Titans are ill-defined, almost shadowy:

> Coeus, the Gyges, and Briareus,
> Typhon, and Dolor, and Porphyrion...
>
> With many more...

and the ministering females, Thea and Moneta, are indefinitely drawn. They may represent all those relatives, ostlers and customers with whom his family had dealings—remote and hard for a child to distinguish from one another.

Here an inexplicable contradiction arises: the conquerors, the newcomers, according to Oceanus, are

> ...eagles golden-feather'd, who do tower
> Above us in their beauty...

yet Hyperion encountered his opponents as "pale Phantoms" "thrice horrible and cold." Apparently conflicting tendencies, longing and suffering confused Keats as he wrote, so that he was relieved to finish abruptly. The poem not only portrays his incipient decrepitude[3] it also shows a lingering retreat to a more secure time—his earliest years. On the other hand, he cannot gainsay the vitality of Apollo, who exclaimed, "Knowledge enormous makes a God of me"—an acknowledgement that creativity depends less on learning, such as familiarity with the classics, and more on empathy for suffering. As Apollo explained,

> Names, deeds, grey legends, dire events, rebellions,
> Majesties, sovran voices, agonies,
> Creations and destroyings, all at once
> Pour into the wide hollows of my brain...

Keats was loath to be superceded; but which side was he on—the ancient authorities or the usupers? When April came, he could endure the indecision no longer. He abandoned *Hyperion* in mid-line.

Three months later he returned to the challenge, to make even more contradictions. The second poem is called *The Fall of Hyperion,* but this is just what he does not do. The poem ends, speaking of Hyperion, with

> ...On he flared.

The poem is described as a dream, but Keats asserts himself as a poet rather than a dreamer:

> Whether the dream now purpos'd to rehearse
> Be poet's or fanatic's will be known
> When this warm scribe my hand is in the grave.

To describe an experience as a dream is to evade responsibility for the happenings, to belittle its actuality. Yet in contrast to the first version of Hyperion's fall, Keats tells this as a participant. He finds,

> ...on a mound
> Of moss, was spread a feast of summer fruits,
> Which, nearer seen, seem'd refuse of a meal
> By angel tasted, or our Mother Eve;
> For empty shells were scattered on the grass,
> And grape-stalks but half bare...

In *Endymion,* in the lurking Keats' early youth, there was one banquet after another, in which Endymion did not join. But this now points to a time when the old, fabulous feasts are over at last. True to form, the lurking Keats falls asleep, protesting that he has been drugged. He awakes and looks around. He sees wrecks and refuse, which reiterates that the dreamer is out of peril, that the fall of the Gods is long since over. The dreamer is threatened with death but overcomes it by climbing steps to an altar—poignant lines to write so soon after December 1, 1818, when John Keats had found Tom stiff and cold in the bed beside his own.

Other conflicting considerations hindered Keats' quill pen and made him contradict himself. His financial assets were uncertain through no fault of his own, his supply of energy diminished by the need to fight off infection. He was reluctant to let the Titans go despite their suffering. He needed someone to take their place, but Apollo was still sleeping on the island of Delos. In the first version Mnemosyne had said to him,

> ...and awaking up
> Didst find a lyre all golden by thy side,
> Whose strings touch'd by thy fingers, all the vast
> Unwearied ear of the whole Universe
> Listen'd in pain and pleasure...

In a letter to George he paraphrased these lines with

> Child, I know thee
> Child no more,
> But a poet evermore

See, see the lyre, the lyre
In a flame of fire
Upon the little cradle's top...

Awake it from its sleep
And see if it can keep
Its eyes upon the blaze...

It puts its little hand into the flame
And on the strings
Paddles a little tune and sings...

Little child o' the western wild,
A Poet now or never!

He was finally able to deal with his feelings about becoming one of the older generation—the suffering Titans—because a new generation was to be born to the Keats family. This infant, for whom he prophesied the achievements he himself had hoped for, was the child of George and Georgiana, due to be born in February 1819. If Keats could identify with this child he could achieve the longed-for closeness to Georgiana, and could exclaim, "O Death, where is thy sting?"

Footnotes for Chapter VII

1 Gittings, *Letters,* p. 51

2 Gittings, *John Keats,* p. 230

3 Coincidentally, Shelley had a similar experience. Mary Shelley told how illness had aged him prematurely: "...thus, during a short life, he had gone through more experience of sensation than many whose existence is protracted. 'If I die tomorrow,' he said, on the eve of his unanticipated death, 'I have lived to be older than my father.'"

Chapter VIII

And when a lady's in the case
You know all other things give place.
John Gay
Fables

Elusively, in and out of Keats' life, there came one Mrs. Isabella Jones. Of her appearance we know little, of her origin even less. No point asking who or where was Mr. Jones. Keats met her in a village near Hastings in the summer of 1817, and as he put it "warmed with her...and kissed her" and hoped to spend "some pleasant hours with her..."[1] Instead they lost touch until by chance they passed each other in a London street. Then she invited Keats to her room, a more sumptuous lodging than those of most of his friends. She sent Tom an expensive gift of grouse to tempt his appetite. Yet she did not encourage further intimacy, though she seems to have been interested in Keats' writing. His publisher, Taylor, was one of her admirers; another was an elderly wealthy Irishman. We catch a glimpse of her in the verses beginning

Hush, hush! tread softly! Hush, hush, my dear!
All the house is asleep, but we know very well
That the jealous, the jealous old bald-pate may hear,
Though you've padded his nightcap, O sweet Isabel!

Nothing furtive or hush-hush about the next woman who intrigued Keats, an orphaned cousin of the Reynolds', Jane Cox, who had come to live with them. Keats described her to George as "not Cleopatra, but at least a Charmian."[2]

She has a rich, Eastern look. She has fine eyes and fine manners. When she comes into a room she makes an impression the same as the beauty of a leopardess. She is too fine and too conscious of herself to repulse any man who may address her. From habit she thinks that nothing particular...I am at such times too much occupied with admiring to be awkward or atremble. I forget myself entirely because I live in her. You will by this time think I am in love with her; so before I go any further I will tell you I am not—She kept me awake one night as a tune of Mozart's might do...[3]

Though images of Isabella and Jane haunted his rest, they only seemed to have appealed to the ostensible Keats. He was content to enjoy their company in an everyday setting—no need to carry them off to Mount Latmos or Florence as he had done in *Endymion* and *The Pot of Basil*.

His basic stance was one of passivity, as when he told Georgiana in a letter,

I should like her [Jane Cox] to ruin me, and I should like you to save me.[4]

Apparently it did not occur to him to play an active role with either.

Keats was ill-prepared for an obssession far more compelling than his involvements with the fair nymphs.

At Tom's death, Keats had moved from his lodging in Well Walk to join Brown at Hampstead. Brown and a couple named Dilke had a double house, Wentworth Place, with a dividing wall and two front doors, set in a lawn among shrubs and shaded by elms and oaks.[5] In contrast to Well Walk, with the chatter of the Bentley children and of visitors to the public fountain, Wentworth Place was quiet except for bird songs and the occasional voices of passing watchmen and vendors. Though near the village, it had a sense of seclusion.

Mrs. Dilke arranged a meeting between Keats and a young girl from nearby Downshire Hill—Fanny Brawne. Fanny's biographer tells that

She was small, her eyes were blue, and often enhanced by blue ribbons in her brown hair. Her mouth expressed determination and a sense of humor, and her smile was disarming. She was not conventionally beautiful; her nose was a little too aquiline, her face too pale and thin—(some called it sallow)—But she knew the value of elegance; velvet hats and muslin bonnets, crepe hats with argus feathers, straw hats embellished with grapes and tartan ribbons: Fanny noticed them all as they came from Paris. She could answer, at a moment's notice, any question on

58

historical costume...The Brawnes possessed a piano and Fanny enjoyed music; her voice was "singularly sweet." She was fond of dancing and moved with natural but cultivated grace...books were her favorite topic of conversation: "There is nothing I like better to talk about, unless it is to such a very great judge that I am afraid they will think all my delightful criticism nonsense."[6]

Keats wrote to his brother in America,

Shall I give you Miss Brawne? She is about my height, with a fine style of countenance of the lengthen'd sort—she wants sentiment in every feature—she manages to make her hair look well —her nostrills are fine—though a little painful—her mouth is bad and good—her Profile is better than her full face which indeed is not full but pale and thin without showing any bone—Her shape is very graceful and so are her movements—her Arms are good, her hands baddish—her feet tolerable—she is not seventeen— but she is ignorant—monstrous in her behavior, flying out in all directions, calling people such names—that I was forced lately to make use of the term Minx—that is I think not from any innate vice but from a penchant she has for acting stylishly. I am however tired of such style and shall decline any more of it.[7]

There was slight chance of any declining, since her home, Elm Cottage, was a haven of feminine domesticity to a lonely young bachelor. Fanny had two special appeals for Keats; her stature did not emphasize his shortness, and ever since he could talk he had loved her name, which was his mother's. The setting of Wentworth Place was ideal for romance—close to the wilderness of the Heath and with Mrs. Dilke's nearby presence as a conventional chaperone. Evidently there were many meetings which have not been recorded in Keats' poetry or correspondence, and they came to an understanding on Christmas Day 1818. It was, Fanny said, the "happiest day" of her life.

The ostensible Keats was ecstatic, yet the lurking Keats was discontented, and rejected the present with a poem that is an appeal for escape:

Ever let the fancy roam,
Pleasure never is at home...
Every thing is spoilt by use:

59

Where's the cheek that doth not fade,
Too much gaz'd at? Where's the maid
Whose lip mature is ever new?
Where's the eye, however blue,
Doth not weary?

Fanny may have been hurt by these lines, and she must have felt aggrieved at Keats' conduct in January. He and Brown were invited to Chichester and Bedhampton by the parents and in-laws of Charles Dilke. As far as we know, Keats was under no obligation to make this trip, a rough and chilly coach-top journey. And though he was a prolific correspondent at other times, the only message from Chichester which has been preserved is a letter written with Brown, with a brief greeting to "Millamant"—his transient nickname for Fanny.

Whether their engagement was official or not, Fanny evidently did not feel herself committed to avoid social obligations, nor did Keats let his anxiety about her prevent him from leaving Hampstead. There is a suggestion of conflict here between Keats' desire for her exclusive company and Fanny's need to maintain her social contacts. It seems improbable that he would have cared to accompany her to the public assemblies in Hampstead, since that would have meant an outlay of money he could ill afford, and possibly investing in smarter clothing than he usually wore. The competition, consisting of officers from nearby barracks and aristocratic refugees from the French Revolution, could have been overwhélming.

Though the ostensible Keats temporarily deserted Fanny, the lurking Keats, writing *The Eve of St. Agnes,* was more energetic and ardent than he had been as Endymion or Lorenzo. As Porphyro, he struggled across the moors to see his love, Madeline. What made this excursion so brave was the weather; even the wild creatures suffered:

St. Agnes' Eve—Ah, bitter chill it was!
The owl, for all his feathers, was a-cold
The hare limp'd trembling through the frozen grass...

Tradition held that on St. Agnes' Eve, January 21st

Young virgins might have visions of delight,
And soft adorings from their loves receive
Upon the honey'd middle of the night,

If ceremonies due they did aright
As, supperless to bed they must retire,
And couch supine their beauties, lilly white
Nor look behind, nor sideways, but require
Of Heaven with upward eyes for all that they desire.

The absent Fanny was assigned the role of Madeline. Keats assuaged his anxiety over her being one of the belles of Hampstead with

...in vain
Came many a tiptoe, amorous cavalier,
And back retir'd; not cool'd by high disdain,
But she saw not; her heart was otherwise...

Keats improved on the legend; when Madeline withdrew from the dance to see her lover, it was not a ghost who came into her room, but Porphyro himself. An elderly pair who helped bring about the meeting —the Beadsman and Angela, the nurse—allowed him to include in the poem his host and hostess, old Mr. and Mrs. Dilke. They took Keats to see the architectural glories of Chichester Cathedral, and these appeared in Madeline's bedroom:

A casement high and triple-arch'd there was,
All garlanded with carven imag'ries
Of fruits, and flowers, an bunches of knot-grass
And diamonded with panes of quaint device,
Innumerable of stains and splended dyes...

...and dim emblazonings,
A shielded scutcheon blush'd with blood of queens and kings.

It would seem that Keats was picturing how Fanny would have looked had she been beside him as he admired the stained glass windows, for he told how the moonlight shining through them

...threw warm gules on Madeline's fair breast,
As down she knelt for heaven's grace and boon;
Rose-bloom fell on her hands, together prest,
And on her silver cross soft amethyst,
And on her hair a glory, like a saint...

Although Madeline was described as having a family hostile to Porphyro, he was not called upon to battle her kin. As they escaped southward, their worst enemy was the "wind's uproar" and the "flaw-blown sleet." Porphyro was the most vital and bold role that the lurking Keats played.

When he was actually with Fanny, back in Hampstead again, the lurking Keats took on a feminine role which exempted him from exertion and initiative; he looked back on his visit to Chichester and wrote *The Eve of St. Mark*. The poem was "quite in the spirit of Town quietude" and of "walking about an old county town on a coolish evening."[8] He had had enough of chill and church services; as Bertha, he stayed by a warm fire and read while the neighbors went to Evensong.

Downshire Hill was near enough to Wentworth Place for Keats and Fanny to see each other often and easily. It is possible that Keats' reaction to these meetings is shown in the *Song of Four Faeries*. Spirits of "Fire, Air, Earth, and Water" pronounce their preferences and aversions. Brown at this time was writing a piece with faery characters, but the main theme of Keats' song is a plea that those with similar tastes should be allowed to hobnob, while those who were uncongenial should stay apart. Although Fanny had declared that books were her favorite topic, her most lively interests were fabrics and styles, a far cry from the Milton and Dante of Keats' concern.

Another use of the faery theme was made at this time in a comical, unfinished extempore sent to George. Here a princess, extravagantly dressed and attended by a dwarf, an ape and a fool, bursts in on the Faeries' Court in their absence. Her attendants warn her against the vengeance of the faeries: "I would not give sixpence for her head," says the dwarf. Many speculations have assigned the originals of these characters to Keats and his brothers: John the dwarf, George the ape, and Tom the fool. And of course Fanny Brawne the princess. The house at Wentworth Place, with Brown concocting pieces concerning faeries, was the Court.

It is difficult to see what satisfaction Keats could have found in caricaturing his family. It must, though, be more than a coincidence that he wrote of an intrusive princess so soon after April 1st, when Mrs. Brawne, Fanny and the two younger children moved into the other side of the Wentworth Place house, which the Dilkes had vacated.[9] Keats and Fanny could not have been closer unless they actually shared the same domicile. With the window open, he heard her singing and playing the piano, and if he looked out he was bound to see her in fashionable elegance starting off to the village shops.

A poem written at this time, *La Belle Dame Sans Merci*, has a possible three-fold origin. An ancient folk tale tells of a youth who spends a night with a faery in opulent surroundings, and wakes to find that it is many years later and that he is an old man. The time of the poem is autumn:

> The sedge is wither'd from the lake
> And no birds sing.

This contradicts the actual season, when every bough had its choir of robins, thrushes and blackbirds. Tom had still been alive the previous autumn, though failing rapidly. His last days had been excited and afterwards bitterly disappointed by love letters from a creature of fancy, Amena Bellefille. She had expressed deep passion for Tom, but was herself the fabrication of several of Keats' friends, especially one Charles Wells. The revelation of the deception, which wounded Tom, infuriated Keats:

> It was no thoughtless hoax, but a cruel deception on a sanguine
> temperament, with every show of friendship...[10]

In the poem the lurking Keats continues to declare himself Fanny's vassal, in thrall to "La Belle Dame Sans Merci," but in doing so, he seems to have identified with his last impressions of Tom,

> So haggard and so woe-begone...
>
> I see a lilly on thy brow,
> With anguish moist and fever dew...

The third origin was his relationship with Fanny, who, although warm and loving, threatened him by stimulating him and encroaching on his concentration for writing, which he considered could make him immortal. Later that year he was to write to her,

> The very first week I knew you I wrote myself your vassal.[11]

La Belle Dame was enormously dangerous, since she had so many victims:

> ...pale kings, and princes too,
> Pale warriors, death-pale were they all
> Who cry'd—"La Belle Dame Sans Merci
> Hath thee in thrall!"

Yet the ardent physical attachment to Fanny persisted, and is told directly in the exquisite *Ode to Psyche*. The ostensible Keats explained his choice of subject in a letter to George:

> You must recollect that Psyche was not embodied as a goddess before the time of Apulieus the Platonist who lived after the Augustan age, and consequently the Goddess was never worshipped or sacrificed to with any of the ancient fervor...I am more orthodox than to let a heathen Goddess be so neglected—[12]

But instead of the glories of ancient Greece, the ode goes on to celebrate a very physical encounter:

> [I] saw two fair creatures, couched side by side
> In deepest grass, beneath the whisp'ring roof
> Of leaves and trembled blossoms, where there ran
> A brooklet, scarce espied...
>
> They lay calm-breathing on the bedded grass;
> Their arms embraced, and their pinions too;
> Their lips touched not, but had not bade adieu,
> As if disjoined by soft-handed slumber,
> And ready still past kisses to outnumber...
>
> The winged boy I knew;
> But who wast thou, O happy, happy dove?
> His Psyche true!

It seems unlikely that Keats is telling of actual dalliance with Fanny, since in Wentworth Place and Hampstead Heath their intimacy would have been more exposed to passersby than propriety would tolerate. However, the lurking Keats promised to give Fanny his all:

So let me be thy choir, and make a moan
Upon the midnight hours;
Thy voice, thy lute, thy pipe, thy incense sweet
From swinged censer teeming;
Thy shrine, thy grove, thy oracle, thy heat
Of pale-mouth'd prophet dreaming.

Yes, I will be thy priest, and build a fane
In some untrodden region of my mind...

And there shall be for thee all soft delight
That shadowy thought can win,
A bright torch, and a casement ope at night,
To let the warm Love in!

Compelling pictures, but they took place in his mind only. What Fanny probably wanted was a neat little house like Elm Cottage, which she had just left. How Keats felt about such domesticity is revealed in a letter written to her a few months later:

> ...I look not forward with any pleasure to what is call'd being set-
> tled in the world; I tremble at domestic cares...[13]

Though Fanny was deeply appreciative of Keats' genius, she must have been impatient at the less practical aspects of his personality, otherwise why would he have written in May,

> Or if thy mistress some rich anger shows,
> Emprison her soft hand, and let her rave,
> And feed deep, deep upon her peerless eyes.[14]

Now the season was coming when Brown habitually left for Scotland and rented his side of Wentworth Place. There were nearby villages galore—Kentish Town, Pinner, Wembley, to name a few—where Keats could have lodged, still close enough to see Fanny fairly easily. Instead he took a trip of many hours to Shanklin, in the Isle of Wight. The place had charmed him two years before, when he had visited there briefly. He had told Reynolds, "Shanklin is a most beautiful place."[15] It was at least three stages by coach to Southampton, and then a boat trip across the Solent. His company was James Rice, a friend and law student, whose illness "made him rather a melancholy companion."[16] Keats did not write to Fanny immediately upon arrival, and when he did, adoration was mixed with diatribes:

> ...what pleasure I might have in living here and breathing and wandering as free as a stag about this beautiful Coast if the remembrance of you did not weigh so upon me. I have never known any unalloy'd Happiness for many days together: the death or sickness of some one has always spoilt my hours—and now when none such troubles oppress me, it is you must confess very hard that another sort of pain haunt me. Ask yourself my love whether you are not very cruel to have so entrammelled me, so destroyed my freedom...For myself I know not how to express my devotion to so fair a form: I want a brighter word than bright, a fairer word than fair.[17]

While avoiding her assiduously, he stated on the 25th of July,

> How I ache to be with you...[18]

Discontent with his own ambivalence is reflected in the sonnet *Bright Star*:

> Bright Star, would I were stedfast as thou art...

> ...still stedfast, still unchangeable,
> Pillow'd upon my fair love's ripening breast...

Keats was so charmed by Fanny that he considered her beautiful, yet he felt himself handicapped with her by being short, shabby, and frustrated financially. Little wonder he became possessive and anxious about her response to other men. He tended to denigrate himself in an unrealistic fashion, even though many other women had found him attractive. In a letter to Fanny he says,

> I am not a thing to be admired...I hold that place among Men which snubnos'd brunettes with meeting eyebrows do among women...[19]

These reactions can be contrasted to the way he had felt about Jane

Cox. As he told George,

> I always find myself more at ease with such a woman. The picture
> before me always gives me a life and animation which I cannot pos-
> sibly feel with anything inferior. I am at such times too much occu-
> pied with admiring to be awkward or atremble.[20]

In the same letter he makes a revealing juxtaposition of Jane Cox with
Georgiana:

> ...as a Man in the world I love the rich talk of a Charmian; as an
> eternal Being I love the thought of you...I should like her to ruin
> me, and I should like you to save me...[21]

In Fanny, the needs of both of Keats' personalities were aroused and
threatened at the same time; as Endymion and Lorenzo his love had
ended in death—and in his ostensible life his poverty and shortness
handicapped his wooing.

Pieces written at this time concern the dire consequences of marriage. *Lamia* tells of a woman enchanted into a serpent—or a serpent
enchanted into a woman. She seduces one of his passive counterparts,
Lycius, by surrounding him with chimerical luxuries. Confronted by a
philosopher denoting Truth, the enchantment fades away:

> ...with a frightful scream she vanish'd:
> And Lycius' arms were empty of delight,
> As were his limbs of life, from that same night.
> On the high couch he lay!—his friends came round—
> Supported him—no pulse, or breath they found,
> And, in its marriage robe, the heavy body wound.

The description of a woman as a snake was an unflattering concept of
Fanny, yet the picture of the serpent was glowing:

> She was a gordian shape of dazzling hue,
> Vermilion-spotted, golden, green, and blue;
> Striped like a zebra, freckled like a pard,
> Eyed like a peacock, and all crimson barr'd;
> And full of silver moons, that, as she breathed,
> Dissolv'd, or brighter shone...

This is reminiscent of Fanny's tastes, as described by her biographer:

> She collected prints of cashmere dresses, tulle mantillas embroid-
> ered with flowers, tunics of Smyrna silk...[22]

At the same time Keats was aspiring to a performance on Drury Lane with his tragedy *Otho the Great,* suggested by Brown. This play has a leading female character with

> ...deep blue eyes—semi-shaded in white lids,
> Finish'd with lashes fine for more soft shade,
> Completed by her twin-arch'd abon brows—
> White temples of exactest elegance...
>
> So perfect, so divine that our poor eyes
> Are dazzled with the sweet proportioning...
>
> Her nostrils, small, fragrant, faery-delicate
> Her lips—I swear no human bones e'er wore
> So taking a disguise...

matching the description of Fanny in his letter to George. The plot of the play hinges on this character's betrayal of Prince Ludolph, who loves her. They both die at the final curtain, echoing the love-death relationship of *Lamia.*

An unfinished drama also written at this time, *King Stephen,* shows the hero, valiant though defeated, being cared for by the Duke of Gloucester, one of Queen Maud's knights. Stephen is described as a doughty fighter. He is comfortably and lovingly provided for in spite of the Queen's hostility, yet he is not safe, since it is observed that

> A Queen's nod
> Can make his June December.

It might seem farfetched to identify these personages as Maud for Fanny and Gloucester for Brown, but it must be more than coincidence that gives these characters roles which correspond in an exaggerated fashion to the situation at Wentworth Place.

Keats moved from Shanklin to Winchester for access to a library needed in writing *Lamia.* Had he gone to London, he would have been near several libraries and Fanny as well, but this he avoided. When he made a brief visit to her in Hampstead, he wrote,

> The day is gone, and all its sweets are gone!
> Sweet voice, sweet lips, soft hand, and softer breast,
> Warm breath, light whisper, tender semi-tone,
> Bright eyes, accomplish'd shape, and lang'rous waist!

"Gone" and "faded" are repeated throughout the poem like the notes of a funeral bell. They were evidently meant to convey a sense of loss, but it would seem that what they really tell is release:

> But, as I've read love's missal through to-day,
> He'll let me sleep, seeing I fast and pray.

After a short stay in Westminster, he returned in mid-October to Wentworth Place. Despite the ups and downs of their relationship, Fanny and Keats were formally engaged at Christmas.

In February 1820 an arterial hemorrhage signalled for Keats his "death warrant." He remained at Wentworth Place, cared for by Fanny and her mother, until September, when he embarked for Italy for a warmer climate on the advice of his doctors. Typically, Fanny did her best for him by lining headgear for the sea journey. Typically, Keats described his reaction to Brown from the boat:

> The silk lining she put in my traveling cap scalds my head...[23]

The lurking Keats had always feared Fanny, since so many of his roles as a lover involved disaster. Endymion's achievement resulted in his disappearance; Lorenzo was murdered; Lycius died on his wedding night, as did Prince Ludolph. A close love relationship was likely to end in death, which he even expressed a desire for:

> I have two luxuries to brood over in my walks, your loveliness and
> the hour of my death. O that I could have possession of them both
> in the same minute...[24]

he had written to Fanny the previous July.

There was, though, a more realistic reason for his dread. Keats felt his existence depended on becoming a well-established poet, both for the financial security it would give him, and for the social status. On hearing that a friend was quoted as saying, "O, he is quite the little Poet," he wrote to George,

> Now this is abominable—you might as well say Buonaparte is quite the little Soldier—you see what it is to be under six foot and not a lord...[25]

To fulfill his poetic potential meant collecting multitudes of beautiful, suitable words, arranging them for eloquent statements, discovering vivid metaphors, and matching melodious rhymes. Before this could be done, he needed to think through and sort out concepts, to evaluate possible topics. These mental activities took a preponderance of his dwindling energy; courting Fanny encroached on this activity and, more demandingly, on his concentration. When he set himself a poetic task, mental glimpses of Fanny slipped in under his closed eyelids, and echoes of her singing broke into his solitude.

> Heard melodies are sweet, but those unheard
> Are sweeter...[26]

he had said. The unheard, persistent songs were indeed too sweet for Keats not to listen to them.

Footnotes for Chapter VIII

1 Gittings, *Letters*, p. 169

2 Cleopatra's attendant in Shakespeare's *Antony and Cleopatra.*

3 Gittings, *Letters*, p. 162

4 Ibid., p. 163

5 A bush whose mulberries Keats and Fanny Brawne enjoyed still bears today.

6 Joanna Richardson, *Fanny Brawne*, (London: The Vanguard Press Inc., 1952) p. 22

7 Ibid., p. 25

8 Gittings, *Letters*, p. 315

9 Mrs. Brawne is reported to have objected to the engagement, but this is contradicted by her moving into Wentworth Place. It may not be unwarranted to impute that Mrs. Brawne, not yet 40, was attracted by the idea of living so close to two bachelors—one, Brown, near her age and comparatively well-to-do, and the other, Keats, who had a magnetic charm and a budding poetic reputation.

10 Gittings, *Letters*, p. 239

11 Ibid., p. 271

12 Ibid., p. 253

13 Ibid., p. 271

14 *Ode on Melancholy*

15 Gittings, *Letters*, p. 5

16 Ibid., p. 267

17 Ibid., p. 263

18 Ibid., p. 270

19 Ibid., p. 271

20 Gittings, *Letters,* p. 162

21 Ibid., p. 163

22 Richardson, *Fanny Brawne,* p. 22

23 Gittings, *Letters,* p. 397

24 Ibid., p. 271

25 Ibid., p. 212

26 *Ode on a Grecian Urn*

Chapter IX

For a desperate disease,
A desperate cure.
                Montaigne •
      The Custom of the Isle of Cea

The two lethal factors which influenced both the ostensible and lurking Keats were, first of all, the tubercle bacillus, and next, the doctors who undertook to deal with it. The situation was exacerbated by mocking critics whose jibes attacked both aspects of Keats' personality; as Shelley said in his Preface to *Adonais—an Elegy on the Death of John Keats,*

> The savage criticism…produced the most violent effect on his
> susceptible mind.

His health had been poor before the Scottish trip, but not yet menacing. The trip debilitated him with exposure and overexertion. Tom's fatal illness was contagious, and Keats did not spare himself in his care of his brother. The tubercle bacillus, once lodged in his lungs and probably in his pharynx, continued to breed and proliferate until it had broken down the walls of blood vessels and left the miniscule gaping wounds that produced hemorrhage. At the same time a toxic secretion poisoned the rest of his system.

Medical tradition at the time ordained that if there was poison in the blood, some of the blood must be extracted so that the patient could better deal with what was left. Armed with this fallacy, members of the Royal College of Surgeons could take away the sources of healing oxygen in the blood supply. At the same time, nourishment to supply the body's defenses was withheld to combat the fever. And there was apparently no restriction on exertion in Keats' case.

Nowadays Keats' life would be prolonged by thorough rest, safeguarding from anxiety, and ample nourishment, but all these were in short supply, making his early doom inevitable.

A forerunner of his physical collapse is the sinister note of debility in his work. This becomes apparent in poems declaring lethargy and inactivity to be desirable, which would appeal to someone whose sources of energy are becoming low. As early as March 1817 he had told of the burden his idealism and creativity laid upon him:

> My spirit is too weak—mortality
> Weighs heavily on me like unwilling sleep,
> And each imagin'd pinnacle and steep
> Of godlike hardship, tells me I must die
> Like a sick Eagle looking at the sky...[1]

In April 1819, in the *Ode on Indolence,* he personified what had been his chief motivations—Love, Ambition, and Poesy—saying,

> ...Ye cannot raise
> My head cool-bedded in the flowery grass;
> For I would not be dieted with praise,
> A pet-lamb in a sentimental farce!
> Fade softly from my eyes, and be once more
> In masque-like figures on the dreamy urn...
>
> Vanish, ye Phantoms! from my idle spright,
> Into the clouds, and never more return!

This declaration of resignation could well be correlated with a physical inability to satisfy the demands of a creative life.

His aversion to energetic behavior was augmented by the fact that the time for summer withdrawal from Wentworth Place was coming near. The move demanded exertion which would tax Keats' strength unbearably. He looked up at the new leaves on the elms and found them a threat, while on the Grecian statuary were

> ...happy, happy boughs! that cannot shed
> Your leaves, nor ever bid the Spring adieu...

At the same time there was a vision of a courtship without change or activity. He addressed

> Fair youth, beneath the trees, thou canst not leave
> Thy song, nor ever can those trees be bare;
> Bold Lover, never, never canst thou kiss,

> Though winning near the goal—yet, do not grieve;
> She cannot fade, though thou hast not thy bliss,
> For ever wilt thou love, and she be fair!

In contrast to his withdrawal from the beauties of life in the *Ode on Indolence,* here is perpetual beauty.

> Thou still unravish'd bride of quietness,
> Thou foster-child of silence and slow time...

is a stark contrast to the dancing, singing, piquant loveliness of Fanny Brawne. This bride is no challenge to his strength.

The same mood of resignation appears in a sonnet on Fame written at this time. The personification is characteristic, and the apparent rejection of what had been so important to him fits his mood of being inadequate to achieve the goal he craved.

To Autumn, written in Winchester in September 1819, evokes an epicene figure

> ...careless on a granary floor,
> Thy hair soft-lifted by the winnowing wind;
> Or on a half-reaped furrow sound asleep...

and surrounded by the minutiae he described so accurately and vividly:

> ...in a wailful choir the small gnats mourn,
> Among the river sallows, borne aloft
> Or sinking as the light wind lives or dies;
> And full-grown lambs loud bleat from hilly bourn;
> Hedge-crickets sing; and now with treble soft
> The red-breast whistles from a garden-croft;
> And gathering swallows twitter in the skies.

The feeling the poem evokes is one of satiation and peace, with no need for further accomplishment—a tranquil loveliness. Such an ambience appeals to someone whose vitality is diminishing.

In quite another context we find regression. In April 1819 Keats had been re-reading Cary's translation of Dante's *Inferno,* and wrote to George,

The Fifth Canto of Dante pleases me more and more—it is that one in which he meets with Paolo and Francesca—I had passed many days in rather a low state of mind, and in the midst of them I dreamt of being in that region of Hell. The dream was one of the most delightful enjoyments I ever had in my life—I floated about the whirling atmosphere as it is described with a beautiful figure to whose lips mine were joined (as) it seem'd for an age—and in the midst of all this cold and darkness I was warm—even flowery tree tops sprung up and we rested on them sometimes with the lightness of a cloud till the wind blew us away again—I tried a Sonnet upon it—there are fourteen lines but nothing of what I felt in it—O that I could dream it every night…

> As Hermes once took to his feathers light
> When lulled Argus, baffled, swoon'd and slept
> So on a delphic reed my idle spright
> So play'd, so charm'd, so conquer'd, so bereft
> The dragon world of all its hundred eyes
> And seeing it asleep so fled away:—
> Not to pure Ida with its snow cold skies,
> Nor unto Tempe where Jove grieved that day,
> But to that second circle of sad hell,
> Where in the gust, the whirlwind and the flaw
> Of Rain and hailstones lovers need not tell
> Their sorrows—Pale were the sweet lips I saw
> Pale were the lips I kiss'd and fair the form
> I floated with about that melancholy storm—

I want very very much a little of your wit my dear Sister—a Letter or two of yours just to bandy back a pun or two across the Atlantic and send a quibble over the Floridas.

After some facetiousness about life in America, Keats instructed Georgiana:

While you are hovering with your dinner in prospect you may do a thousand things—put a hedgehog into George's hat—pour a little water into his rifle—soak his boots in a pail of water—cut his jacket round into shreds like a roman kilt or the back of my grandmothers stays—Sow *off* his buttons…[2]

The dream he relates in this letter harks back to Endymion, who was "lapp'd and lull'd along the dangerous sky" and indicates a regression to an earlier stage of life. It was the moon goddess in whose arms he had lain, and now it was an unnamed "beautiful figure to whose lips mine were joined." He stresses the pallor of her lips. This is an unusual, if not a contradictory adjective for lips. In the sonnet to Georgiana, Keats had described her lips as "ruby," in Extracts from an Opera, "my lady's cherry lips," and when he begged someone "O love me truly!" her lips were "coral tinted." But paleness he associated with the breast, and spoke of Fanny Brawne's "warm, white, lucent, million-pleasured breast," which would take him back to Endymion again; if it was the breast, he was not the mate of that "fair form" but her baby. The dream takes place in the circle of Hell where Dante met Paolo and Francesca Da Rimini. Keats had just read about this and was dreaming himself as Paolo with his sister-in-law. Georgiana was about to have her first child, and it would seem that Keats, all unaware, was dreaming himself in the child's place. The dream has two benefits to the dreamer: he is committing incest with the sister-in-law he loves, and he is warm in the midst of cold and darkness—a miraculous and much to be desired happening. The dream shows reaction to the weather in describing the second circle of Hell according to Dante:

> I came into a place void of all light, which bellows like the sea in tempest, when it is combated by warring winds.

> The hellish storm, which never rests, leads the spirits with its sweep; whirling, and smiting it vexes them.[3]

Sounds of a storm must have penetrated Keats' sleep that night, for he wrote in the same journal entry, "There is a north wind blowing, playing young gooseberry with the trees." The extreme enjoyment which this dream gave to him shows a great need to retreat to an easier time of life, and bygone loves.

Another evidence of deteriorated energy appears in the satire *The Cap and Bells,* which Keats wrote in the mornings during November and December 1819. Brown recollected that he composed it with the greatest facility. In one instance Brown copied as many as twelve stanzas before dinner. So rich and so fluent are the 88 stanzas of this topical satire that it is easy to overlook the degradation of its characters. They are puny, trivial, petulant and tyrannical; faeries rather than humans.

There is tremendous contrast between these and the Titans, the Gods, and even the characters of Madeline and Bertha. It is as though Keats had to degrade those he wrote about, and had less idealization and respect. About the same time, he wrote a fragment called Gripus, which was also belittling and rather ugly.

In the debate on the time when Keats' terminal illness began, Sir William Hale-White considered he was healthy until his closeness to the moribund, infectious Tom on his return from Scotland.[4] Yet he felt unwell before the Scottish trip, and what he endured there was certainly deleterious. Without joining in diagnostic squabbles, we can point out unacknowledged signs of ill health in his writing, particularly his frequent mention of coldness. Cold represented to Keats a menacing world and the ultimate horror of death. What would seem pleasantly cool to the touch of most people, shocked him with chill. In Endymion, for instance, he wrote of

> Brimming the lilly cups with tears
> Cold as my fears

and warned

> Speak not of grief, young stranger, or cold snails
> Will slime the rose tonight.

When Glaucus told young Endymion of meeting his dead love,

> ...Cold, O cold indeed
> Were her fair limbs.

Endymion speculated on what terrors Glaucus had in store for him:

> What lonely death am I to die
> In this cold region? Will he let me freeze
> And float my brittle limbs o'er polar seas?

Hyperion in his downfall cried,

> ...O effigies of pain,
> O spectres busy in a cold cold gloom...

So at Hyperion's words the Phantoms pale
Bestirr'd themselves, thrice horrible and cold.

In St. Agnes' Eve the prime enemy Porphyro braved was the weather: "flaw-blown sleet." Shock at the touch of cold is a sign of a raised temperature. It could well indicate an intermittent, subclinical fever, which Keats mentions often in his correspondence but appears not to have taken seriously. Another sign of long-standing enervation is his preference for the verb floating or flitting, which denotes an effortless movement while supported or carried.

For a while his debility favored the lurking Keats. Cut off from activity, his emotions and notions found expression in his imagination. It was the ostensible Keats that his well-meaning physicians inadvertently murdered. We follow with horror news of this prolonged and painful tragedy: the anxious tedium at Wentworth Place, while Mrs. Brawne and Fanny cared for him; the tormented speculation about whom Fanny was meeting every time he saw her go through the garden gates, as shown in his verse,

> Who now, with greedy looks, eats up my feast?
> What stare outfaces now my silver moon!
> Ah! keep that hand unravish'd at the least;
>   Let, let the amorous burn—
>   But pr'ythee, do not turn
> The current of your heart from me so soon.
>   O! save, in charity,
>   The quickest pulse for me.
>
> Save it for me, sweet love! though music breathe
> Voluptuous visions into the warm air;
> Though swimming through the dance's dangerous wreath,
>   Be like an April day
>   Smiling and cold and gay
> A temperate lilly, temperate as fair;
>   Then, Heaven! there will be
>   A warmer June for me.

and the reproaches:

> This living hand, now warm and capable

Of earnest grasping, would, if it were cold
And in the icy silence of the tomb,
So haunt thy days and chill thy dreaming nights
That thou wouldst wish thine own heart dry of blood
So in my veins red life might stream again,
And thou be conscience-calmed—see here it is—
I hold it towards you.

the harrassment of ill-managed funds beyond his control; the slings and arrows of outrageous reviewers; the repeated threat of blood-stains after a cough; the ensuing weakness, augmented by members of the Royal College of Surgeons opening his veins; the gnawing hunger, provoked by a diet "a mouse would starve upon..."[5] Finally, there was the anguish of parting from Fanny for his trip to Italy. Once aboard the brigantine *Maria Crowther,* with its damp, cramped cabin, he could not bear to write to Fanny herself. He poured out his heart to Brown:

> The persuasion that I shall see her no more will kill me...I should
> have had her when I was in health, and I should have remained
> well. I can bear to die—I cannot bear to leave her. O, God! God!
> God! Everything I have in my trunks that reminds me of her
> goes through me like a spear...My imagination is horribly vivid
> about her—I see her—I hear her. I am afraid to write to her...to
> see her handwriting would break my heart...If I had any chance
> of recovery, this passion would kill me.[6]

After the frustration of ten days' quarantine delay in Naples came the discomfort and exhaustion of the final drive to Rome; the view of the Roman crowds surging up and down the Spanish Steps; the longing for the relief of death.

On February 23, 1821 relief came. Keats was taken to lie under daisies in the Protestant Cemetery. He said that he should be memorialized with

> Here lies one whose name was writ in water.

In distant Hampstead, a blue-eyed young girl, who considered clothes a paramount means of self-expression, put on deep mourning.

Footnotes for Chapter IX

1 *On Seeing the Elgin Marbles*

2 Gittings, *Letters,* pp. 239-241

3 Dante Alighieri, *The Divine Comedy* (Carlyle Wicksteed Translation)

4 William Hale-White, *Keats as Doctor and Patient,* (London: Oxford University Press, 1938), p. 49

5 Gittings, *Letters,* p. 355

6 Ibid., p. 396

Chapter X

He is a portion of the loveliness
That once he made more lovely.
Shelley
Adonais

The epitaph Keats made for himself—one whose name was writ in water—was so excruciatingly bitter that it revealed the depths of his despair. He had always correlated a reputation as a poet with longevity, even with immortality. As early as 1816 he had written to George,

These are the living pleasures of the bard;
But richer far posterity's reward.
What does he murmur with his latest breath,
While his proud eye looks through the film of death?
"What though I leave this dull, this earthly mould,
"Yet shall my spirit lofty converse hold
"With after times...

In a mood that was lighter but just as sincere, he pictured the posthumous triumph of poets:

Bards of Passion and of Mirth,
Ye have left your souls on earth!
Have ye souls in heaven too,
Double lived in regions new?

If he could be a poet, death would have no sting, and he could contemplate it with resignation:

After dark vapours have oppress'd our plains
For a long dreary season, comes a day
Born of the gentle South, and clears away
From the sick heavens, all unseemly stains.

The calmest thoughts come round us; as of leaves

Budding—fruit ripening in stillness...
...a smiling infant's breath—
The gradual sand that through an hour-glass runs—
A woodland rivulet—a Poet's death.

For the lurking Keats poetry was not just an intellectual exercise; he needed to be totally absorbed in it. He said to Reynolds in 1817:

I find that I cannot exist without poetry—without eternal poetry
—half the day will not do—the whole of it—I began with a little,
but habit has made me a Leviathan.[1]

He pictured the poetic state when he spent the night in Leigh Hunt's study:

It has a glory, and naught else can share it:
The thought thereof is awful, sweet, and holy,
Chasing away all worldliness and folly...

O for ten years, that I may overwhelm
Myself in poesy; so I may do the deed
That my own soul has to itself decreed.[2]

He speculated frequently on what was the poetic role, confiding to Richard Woodhouse in 1818,

As to the poetical character itself...it is not itself—it has no self
—it is everything and nothing...What shocks the virtuous philosopher delights the chameleon poet. It does no harm from its
relish of the dark side of things any more than from its taste for
the bright one; because they both end in speculation. A poet is
the most unpoetical of any thing in existence; because he has no
identity—he is continually in for—and filling some other body.[3]

He made rules for himself, which he told to his publisher, Taylor:

In poetry I have a few axioms, and you will see how far I am from
their centre. First, I think poetry should surprise by a fine ex-
cess and not by singularity—it should strike the reader as a
wording of his own highest thoughts, and appear almost a re-

membrance—second, its touches of beauty should never be half way thereby making the reader breathless rather than content: the rise, the progress, the setting of imagery should like the sun come natural to him—shine over him and set soberly although in magnificence leaving him in the luxury of twilight—but it is easier to think what peotry should be than to write it—and this leads me on to another axiom. That if poetry comes not as naturally as the leaves to a tree it had better not come at all.[4]

The ostensible Keats, before his health gave way, was energetic; not only did he take long walks as was the custom at the time, but he played cricket, and once fought for over an hour with a butcher's boy who was abusing a kitten. The life of the lurking Keats was equally strenuous:

I went day by day at my poem for a month—at the end of which time the other day I found my brain so overwrought that I had neither rhyme nor reason in it...[5]

he told Taylor. In another letter to his publishers, he asserted independence:

Had I been nervous about its being a perfect piece...and with that view asked advice...it would not have been written; for it is not in my nature to fumble—I will write independently...the genius of poetry must work out its own salvation in a man...that which is creative must create itself...[6]

He encouraged himself in his calling, with

Where's the poet? show him! show him,
Muses nine! that I may know him!
'Tis the man who with a man
Is an equal, be he King,
Or poorest of the beggar-clan...

Defending his own work, he said to Reynolds,

Poetry should be great and unobtrusive, a thing which enters into one's soul, and does not startle it, or amaze it with itself, but with its subjects...I don't mean to deny Wordsworth's grandeur and Hunt's merit, but I mean to say we need not be teazed with grandeur and merit when we can have them uncontaminated and unobtrusive...[7]

The ostensible Keats wrote poems of admiration in a straightforward manner, but the lurking Keats could express himself most freely about actual people by placing them in imagined situations and assigned personalities: his family were the classic deities, then Georgiana became Isabella, Fanny was Madeline and again, Lamia. At the same time he could personify abstractions and treat them like people, as he did in the *Ode on Indolence,* when the three figures—Love, Ambition, and Poetry—move past him. And just as he had seen himself as Meg Merrilies and Lycidas, so he identified with the nightingale that sang in the great trees that overshadowed Wentworth Place. He starts with an admission of his physical state,

> My heart aches, and a drowsy numbness pains
> My sense, as though of hemlock I had drunk,
> Or emptied some dull opiate to the drains
> One minute past, and Lethe-wards had sunk...

The nightingale, on the other hand, sings of summer "in full-throated ease." Full-throated is a heartbreaking adjective for a man whose own throat pained with every gulp. He briefly considers wine as a possible remedy, but feels this would be useless. He contrasts the nightingale in the trees with his own saddening experiens, picturing again the people huddled in the outpatient department of a hospital:

> The weariness, the fever and the fret
> Here, where men sit and hear each other groan;
> Where palsy shakes a few, sad, last gray hairs,
> Where youth grows pale, and spectre-thin, and dies...

As a poet, he could escape with the nightingale:

> Not charioted by Bacchus and his pards,
> But on the viewless wings of poesy,
> Though the dull brain perplexes and retards:
> Already with thee! tender is the night,
> And haply the Queen-Moon is on her throne...

In the darkness he pictures his surroundings,

> I cannot see what flowers are at my feet,
> Nor what soft incense hangs upon the boughs,
> But, in embalmed darkness, guess each sweet
> Wherewith the seasonable month endows
> The grass...
>
> The coming musk-rose, full of dewy wine,
> The murmurous haunt of flies on summer eves.

Describing his own situation again, he says,

> Darkling, I listen: and, for many a time
> I have been half in love with easeful Death,
> Call'd him soft names in many a mused rhyme...
> Now more than ever seems it rich to die,
> To cease upon the midnight with no pain,
> While thou art pouring forth thy soul abroad
> In such an ecstasy!

If he felt at one with the nightingale, his immortality was proven:

> Thou wast not made for death, immortal Bird!
> No hungry generations tread thee down;
> The voice I hear this passing night was heard
> In ancient days by emperor and clown:
> Perhaps the self-same song that found a path
> Through the sad heart of Ruth, when, sick for home,
> She stood in tears amid the alien corn;
> The same that oft-times hath
> Charm'd magic casements, opening on the foam
> Of perilous seas, in faery lands forlorn.[8]

The thought of forlorness is alien to the lurking Keats and belies his fancy as though they were mere dreams:

> ...the fancy cannot cheat so well
> As she is fam'd to do...

Was it a vision, or a waking dream?
Fled is that music:—Do I wake or sleep?

He picked up the dream theme again in *The Fall of Hyperion*. He would seem to have been concerned as to the validity of the lurking Keats' visions—whether they were simply frail imaginary structures, or a solace to humanity:

Fanatics have their dreams, wherewith they weave
A paradise for a sect; the savage too
From forth the loftiest fashion of his sleep
Guesses at Heaven; pity those who have not
Trac'd upon vellum or wild Indian leaf
The shadows of their melodious utterance.
But bare of laurel they live, dream, and die;
For Poesy alone can tell her dreams,
With the fine spell of words alone can save
Imagination from the sable chain
And dumb enchantment. Who alive can say,
"Thou art no poet—may'st not tell thy dreams?"
Since every man whose soul is not a clod
Hath visions, and would speak, if he had loved,
And been well nurtured in his mother tongue.
Whether the dream now purpos'd to rehearse
Be poet's or fanatic's will be known
When this warm scribe my hand is in the grave.

The lurking Keats was a keen observer and a logical thinker, able to create new worlds from scraps of memory to take the place of less attractive ambiences. This distinguished him from the ostensible Keats, whose life was spent battling untoward forces. The second self-image is not to be confused with a pathological double personality. There were no stigmata of mental impairment, no loss of memory, no delusional emotions. The signal difference between the lurking and ostensible Keats was the method and focus of their creativity. The ostensible poet was very much a man of his time, dining out, playing cricket, visiting his friends, and attending lectures and exhibits. The lurking Keats existed in fantasied Mediterranean countries—Greece, Delos, Florence. As he wrote to George,

> I feel more and more every day, as my imagination strengthens,
> that I do not live in this world alone but in a thousand worlds.[9]

It was by this self-image that Keats was able to perfect the magnificent harvest of a few short years—1816 to 1819.

The lurking Keats triumphantly achieved his immediate goals. He was able to be his mother's mate without the punishment which was inflicted on Oedipus for the same deed; he was able to make love to Georgiana in the "second circle of sad Hell" without losing his brother's affection; he transmuted the privations of Scotland into pleasures; he achieved stature as Porphyro; and he was able to win Fanny away from more eligible suitors. All these he could gain even while the ostensible Keats was too poverty-stricken and debilitated for activity.

The ostensible Keats was not conscious of allowing his lurking counterpart to take over; it happened spontaneously. Keats seems to have been unaware of which side of his personality was dominant. Yet it is evident that he was happiest while lurking rather than ostensible. The lurking Keats achieved to a large extent the great goal for which he had been created. The ostensible Keats lay in the Protestant Cemetery in Rome, but the prophecy of the lurking Keats has come true: "I think I shall be among the English Poets after my death."[10] He lives for us today as much as he did for his contemporaries nearly two centuries ago.

A thing of beauty is a joy forever.

Footnotes for Chapter X

1 Gittings, *Letters,* p. 7

2 *Sleep and Poetry*

3 Gittings, *Letters,* p. 157

4 Ibid., p. 69

5 Ibid., p. 16

6 Ibid., p. 155

7 Ibid., p. 61

8 *Ode to a Nightingale*

9 Gittings, *Letters,* p. 170

10 Ibid., p. 161

Selected Bibliography

Allott, Miriam, ed. *The Poems of John Keats,* New York: W. W. Norton & Company, 1970.

Forman, H. Buxton, ed., rev. M. Buxton Forman. *The Letters of John Keats,* London: Oxford University Press, 1947.

Gittings, Robert. *John Keats.* Boston: Little, Brown & Company, 1968.

Gittings, Robert, ed. *Letters of John Keats.* London: Oxford University Press, 1938.

Hale-White, Sir William, *Keats as Doctor and Patient.* London: Oxford University Press, 1938.

Richardson, Joanna. *Fanny Brawne.* London: The Vanguard Press, 1952.

About the Author

Geraldine Pederson-Krag, a practicing psychoanalyst for over 40 years, is the author of *Personality Factors in Work and Employment* and numerous papers and reviews in analytic journals. In the course of her private practice she has analyzed a number of well-known literary figures. She is a Member of the Royal College of Surgeons of England, a Licentiate of the Royal College of Physicians of London, a Life Fellow of the American Psychiatric Association and a Life Member of the American Psychoanalytic Association. Dr. Pederson-Krag is the founder of the mental health clinic at Huntington, New York which now bears her name.

Julie Castle is a writer living in Huntington, New York.